Wild & Wise is for ⟨...⟩
Sacred Feminine. Amy Bammel Wilding's meditations can easily be used in women's circles to deepen each woman's connection to goddess archetypes and to yearnings in herself. The questions for deeper reflection can be done alone or shared in the circle. This rich resource is an answer to "what can we do to go deeper?" that many in circles want to know.

— **Jean Shinoda Bolen, MD author of *The Millionth Circle* and *Goddesses in Everywoman***

Sweetly rich and soulfully deep, these beautiful, spot-on meditations have been sorely needed. Wild & Wise will live in my treasure chest of sacred tools to access often for personal use as well as women's circles.

— **Suzanne Mathis McQueen, author of *4 Seasons in 4 Weeks***

Wild & Wise vibrates with revolutionary energy! In these pages, Amy Bammel Wilding shines a brilliant light into the deeper consciousness of women, calling her readers into effortless awareness and greater compassion for both self and others. As a women's circle facilitator, this indispensable source has become my go-to guide, carrying my circles of women into the realm of true transformation time after time. Wild & Wise is essential reading for any woman drawn to looking inward, and all who wish to dance with their own inner wild and wise selves.

— **Melia Keeton-Digby, author of *The Heroines Club: A Mother-Daughter Empowerment Circle***

Through beautifully written, skillfully crafted meditations, filled with reverence and tenderness, Amy Bammel Wilding guides us on a journey to find Holy Sanctuary in ourselves again as women – vital for us and for our times. Wild & Wise is a book to cherish and revisit many times over.

– Alexandra Pope and Sjanie Hugo Wurlitzer, co-authors of *Wild Power: discover the magic of the your menstrual cycle and awaken the feminine path to power*

Wild & Wise offers a powerful sacred journey of initiation for women worldwide, rooted in the wisdom of feminine rites-of-passage. Amy Bammel Wilding opens the doorway to the lost feminine soul, and skillfully shines the light of remembrance. May all women discover this sanctuary within and rebirth their true essence.

– Seren Bertrand, co-author of *Womb Awakening – Initiatory Wisdom from the Creatrix of All Life*

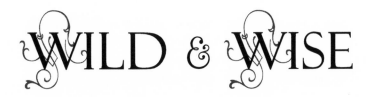

WILD & WISE

Sacred Feminine Meditations for
Women's Circles & Personal Awakening

AMY BAMMEL WILDING

WOMANCRAFT PUBLISHING

Typeset and design by Lucent Word, Co. Cork, Ireland

Published by Womancraft Publishing, 2017
www.womancraftpublishing.com

ISBN: 978-1-910559-376

A percentage of Womancraft Publishing profits are invested back into the environment reforesting the tropics (via TreeSisters) and forward into the community: providing books for girls in developing countries, and affordable libraries for red tents and women's groups around the world.

Womancraft Publishing is committed to sharing powerful new women's voices, through a collaborative publishing process. We are proud to midwife this work, however the story, the experiences and the words are the author's alone.

For my sisters

ACKNOWLEDGEMENTS

This book has been many years in the making, and would not have been birthed into the world without the encouragement and support of my family, friends, and community. To you, I offer my deepest gratitude and most sincere appreciation.

My family – Jason, Brynn, and Soren. You inspire me to be the best version of myself and to make the world a better place. I could not share my medicine with the world in the way that I do without your constant love, encouragement, and support. I love you more!

My father – Carl Sack. Thank you for loving me unconditionally, not in spite of my wildness, but because of it. Thank you for instilling within me the wisdom that I could do and be anything I could imagine, and for the ability to work hard to achieve my goals.

My best friend and life partner – Melia Keeton-Digby. I would not have birthed this book had it not been for your brilliant example and constant encouragement. Your sisterhood is the most profound gift of my life, and has helped shape me into the woman I am. Thank you for always reminding me to shine!

My Red Tent Louisville Sisterhood – without you, these meditations would not have been written. It is because of our magical circle that I was continually inspired to keep writing; it is because of the safe and sacred space we co-create that I knew I could venture so courageously

i

into uncharted territory. I offer my profound and humble gratitude to all of the women who have sat in circle with me. Thank you for trusting me with your journey. Very special thanks to Jill Adelson and Mehrunissa Hassan – it is because of your continued encouragement and love that I allowed myself to imagine sharing the power and intimacy of our meditation experiences with the world. Thank you for believing in me.

My village – Heather Molina, Emily McCay, Kri Martin, Holly Clark, Jen Shean, Tina Meredith, Erica Millard, Paige Waggoner, and Rebecca Cohen. Your friendship and sincere encouragement have sustained and nourished my spirit more than words can say. I am forever grateful for your love and wisdom through the highs and lows of this season of my life, and for supporting me in countless ways as I have worked to manifest my dreams. I am so very blessed to call you my tribe.

My Full Moon Circle sisters – Tina Meredith, Christy Ramos, Erica Coulter, Buffy Troncin, Autumn Grasty, Amy Adams, Lisa Mascio-Thompson, Rhonda Russ, and Nicole Navarra. I would not be who I am today without our many nights around the fire under the full moon. With you, I learned the immense power of women's circles, and it changed my life. Thank you all for being my teachers.

The Wise Women – Jean Shinoda Bolen, Lucy Pearce, Amy Sophia Marashinsky, Suzanne Mathis McQueen, Clarissa Pinkola Estés, Sue Monk Kidd, Pema Chödrön, Starhawk, Tami Lynn Kent, and Christiane Northrup. Your vision, wisdom, and insight have been invaluable throughout my journey; your words have deeply nourished and inspired me. I would not be who I am were it not for your work. Thank you for sharing your gifts with the world.

Contents

INTRODUCTION

Dear sister,

The book you are holding in your hands is not merely a collection of written words, but a powerful tool for personal and global transformation. The meditations within beckon you to explore the powerful realm of symbolism and archetypes, inviting you to access your wild and wise inner knowing – an aspect of your psyche that has likely been suppressed and invalidated throughout your life.

Regardless of where on the planet you live, your experiences as a female in the twentieth and twenty-first centuries have no doubt been shaped by the dominant cultural paradigm: patriarchy. Ubiquitous and toxic to all members of society, patriarchy is a belief system and social structure that perpetuates and rewards actions and attitudes in alignment with the hyper-masculine values of domination, hierarchy, violence, power and male authority. In contrast, the attributes commonly associated with the Sacred Feminine – wisdom, intuition, nurturing, collaboration, respect for life and creation, authenticity, equality, rhythmicity, empowered embodiment, and peace – are devalued and marginalized, leaving all members of our culture, female and male alike, disconnected from an essential aspect of our true nature, and fundamentally incomplete.

For over a decade, I have worked intimately with

women and girls intent on reawakening and reconnecting with the Sacred Feminine – the divine power, sovereignty, and wisdom innate in all women – and have witnessed the profound healing that occurs when women are provided with the language, tools, and support for this transformation. The meditations that I have written have been a crucial key to the life-changing shifts I have witnessed again and again in my women's circles and mother-daughter circles.

The meditations within these pages reflect my own personal awakening and transformation as a woman, a daughter, and a mother, and were written to inspire and guide the girls and women of my community, the Red Tent Louisville sisterhood. Honoring the repeated requests from women the world over to share my medicine, it is with devotion to the awakening of the Sacred Feminine that I now share these meditations with you and the women of your sisterhood.

HOW TO USE THIS BOOK

Whether using this book for a women's group that you facilitate or for your own personal journey of awakening, you will be stepping through a gateway to an inner landscape rich with symbolism and archetypal wisdom each time you are guided through a meditation. Beyond the linear and logical thoughts of the rational mind, each journey will invite you to access your own deep inner knowing, connecting you to your Sacred Feminine core that exists in a realm beyond words.

The transformational power of these meditations is most potent when you allow yourself to be completely held in the experience; much like we cannot dream while we are awake, we cannot fully sink into the realm of the meditative terrain while our conscious mind is still active. For this reason, you will get the most out of the experience by listening to rather than reading the meditations. If you are sharing these meditations with a women's circle or mother-daughter circle, you may wish to first record yourself reading the meditation and then experience it as a listener before guiding your community through the process at a later time. Alternatively, you may wish to record the meditation and then listen to it together with your circle sisters in order to share the experience together.

If you've chosen this book for your own personal journey of awakening and transformation, I recommend recording yourself reading the meditation, and then listening to it when you know you will not be interrupted. Giving yourself the time and space to fully disengage your logical brain will allow you to reap the richest benefit from each meditation.

If you would prefer to be guided by a voice other than your own, an audio recording of these meditations, read by me, is available for purchase on Audible and iTunes, and on CD from Amazon as well as the Red Tent Louisville website (www.redtentlouisville.com) and the Womancraft Publishing website (www.womancraftpublishing.com).

The meditations in this book are organized into three sections. The first contains journeys that invite you to access the realm of the Sacred Feminine within yourself, perhaps for the first time. The second section contains meditations inspired by the Goddess archetype, the characteristics of whom can be found in every woman.

The third section focuses on meditations that celebrate and honor our connection with the natural world and the rhythms of the seasons. Though categorized as such, the universal theme of all of the meditations is a deep reverence for our unique female experience.

Each meditation is followed by three questions, inviting you to spend time in deeper reflection of your experience. Your process may include pondering these questions silently or journaling a response. If you are facilitating a women's circle, the questions may be offered as discussion prompts for your group.

You will also find several meditations that integrate writing into the meditation itself; these will be marked with this pencil icon. You can best prepare for the writing meditation by placing your journal and pen nearby before you begin. If you are listening to a recording of the meditation, pause the recording when you are prompted to begin writing, and then resume the recording when your writing process is complete.

The sequence of the meditations mirrors my own personal journey of awakening and transformation, and you may wish to follow them as they are laid out in this book. However, I am a faithful believer in the intuitive process of evolution, and invite you to tune in with your inner wise woman to see where she would like to go on any given day. There is no wrong path to take. I will emphasize, too, that the meditations in this book are not meant to be experienced just once; you will find that your meditative journey may be vastly different when experienced for a second or even third time, and that with each listening, you are able to connect more deeply and profoundly into your inner wild and wise self.

The power of the meditative journey is not just in the experience itself, but in the cumulative process of regularly accessing of your symbolic and archetypal mind. As you become more practiced in connecting with this aspect of yourself, you will become more and more aware of the messages that your inner wise woman communicates to you on a regular basis. You will feel more connected; more complete. You will cultivate a relationship with your inner world that will be a safe place to return to again and again. You will experience a deep healing, unlike anything that can be offered by another person – because this healing will come from *within*. And to be sure: your personal wholeness and healing is vital and needed now, perhaps more than ever... for when women heal, the world heals.

I've never been patient enough for meditation. The guided meditations in circle have really transformed my life. Sometimes you need someone to guide you to the parts of yourself you're afraid to go to alone.

— EMILY CORBETT

Amy's meditations invite each woman to find her own inner goddess and to walk a path of personal wisdom and healing.

— RAYSUN FROST

Amy's meditations remind us all that the gift of restoration ebbs and flows in the rhythm of our cycles and that we have the ability to tap into our wild wisdom to find the strength to change and heal. I went from a life of chaos and darkness to a life of light and strength by experiencing Amy's medicine.

— HOLLY GOODYEAR

To say that my personal experiences with meditations and talking circles in the Red Tent have been transformative is an understatement. I have come to understand that I have more in common with other women than I thought, and have seen that the power we all have when we combine forces is amazing.

— AMANDA KINAID

These meditations invite all those present to go deeper into themselves to discover precious grains of truth, and to step intentionally into and through their healing journeys.

— MEHRUNISSA HASSAN

I was to be forty in two months and had it not been for the gift of Amy's meditation I could not have marched towards that magical turning of time for myself in wholeness. I was unconditionally connected with the wisdom I needed and the forgiveness I sought. And there was no longer grief. And I was at peace for the first time in a long while. That September night was just one of many nights Amy's voice would bring me to awareness and reconciliation; one of many that I chose life by heeding the call to sisterhood and the sacred feminine.

— JESSICA BEAL

I feel like all the facets of me are evolving as I go deeper into our meditations. As a human, as a woman, a mother, daughter, sister, friend, lover, partner, and more. The meditations connect me to myself, the part of me that feels infinite.

— MANDY CLARK

Amy's meditations have been an amazing help in connecting to the inner me. Through them, I have learned so much: to soothe my Warrior, whose hypervigilance was hampering my ability to trust; to honor the journeys of the Maiden I once was and the Mother I am now; to feel mothered even after the loss of my own mother here on earth; and to connect with the Crone as I look ahead to my journey through perimenopause and menopause. I feel more grounded, more centered and more loved.

— MICHELLE SMITH PIERCE

Growing up, I was taught not to pay attention to my feelings, to stuff them down, to ignore them, to believe that what others wanted or needed or expected of me was more important than my own wants, needs, and feelings.

I have always been great at taking care of others, but have struggled to take care of myself. Thanks to Amy, her meditations, and the women of The Red Tent, I am writing a new story. The meditations help me to get out of my head and into my heart, to really get in touch with what is going on for me on a deeper level.

— GINNY DELANEY

PART I
THE SACRED FEMININE

ORIGINS

These are unquestionably dark times in which we are living. The advances for women and the environment that were hard won over the last century have been seemingly erased with the pen stroke of the current dominant hyper-masculine regime. Our world is out of balance, and this disharmony is echoed by the personal imbalance we all experience as members of a patriarchal society.

The Sacred Feminine is needed in our world now more than ever – on a global level, and on an individual level – to bring our planet and our psyches back into balance. The reawakening and reclaiming of the Divine, by women and for women, began in the last century and is gaining momentum with each passing year. Women the world over, like individual drops in the ocean, are coalescing to form a great wave of change, and the tide is now turning – away from the patriarchal rule this planet has known for over 2000 years.

As is the case with the majority of movements that pertain to women, this shift is coming not from the top down, but from the bottom up. Like seeds buried generations ago, we rise organically, sensing the time is now to see ourselves as the awesome force of nature we were born to be.

The rebirth of the Sacred Feminine is, like most things symbolically female, circular. Rejecting the current social values placed on hierarchy and linearity, women have begun to reclaim the domain of sacred circling as our birthright, honoring our cyclical nature. Women's circles and mother-daughter circles are perhaps the most powerful agents of change on the planet right now, with each woman contributing to the healing of our world as she herself experiences healing.

The meditations in this section were written for my Red Tent women's circles as an invitation to awaken to the toxic reality of patriarchy and to reclaim our inherent sacredness. Each meditation addresses a specific way in which we women have been systematically disconnected from our wholeness, and our holiness, by the oppression and amputation of the Sacred Feminine.

Individually, the meditations offer precise medicine for targeted healing. As a complete collection, they offer profound personal transformation.

And transformation *is* on the horizon, to be sure. As each woman reclaims the power and wisdom of the Sacred Feminine on an individual level, she increases the vibration for all women on a planetary level. The birth of a new era is imminent, and we can have faith that the darkness we perceive in this current time is, in the words of Valarie Kaur, "not the darkness of the tomb, but the darkness of the womb."

COMING HOME

hat would it be like if our life experience as females was that of being safe, being valued, being respected? For many of us, it is difficult to envision being part of a culture in which girls are encouraged to grow into their sovereignty, where women's bodies are trusted and honored; where the Sacred Feminine is valued and cultivated. And while there is not such a place on Earth at this moment in time, we can connect with the energetic vibration of such a reality by creating a collective vision of what it would look like, and perhaps more importantly, what it would feel like. When we tap into the wild and wise potential of the Sacred Feminine, we come home to our deepest truth.

MEDITATION

Close your eyes, and as you deeply inhale and exhale, allow yourself to feel heavy and fully supported. With another inhale and exhale, sink even further into relaxation as you prepare to journey to another space and time. With the freedom to navigate this journey, your spirit knows intuitively exactly where to take you. Using your eternal and unfailing connection to the Sacred Feminine as a compass, your spirit has brought you to a place where women are safe, and life is sacred.

A place of harmonious community, of equality and peace. You observe all that is around you, and see the many girls and women in their glorious diversity. You sense immediately their comfort in their own bodies; the sovereign strength they claim as their birthright. Every day in countless ways, women claim their due space, and their unique ability to create and nurture life is sacred. You know without being told that this is a place where women weave a tapestry of ritual and identity for and with each other. For and with their mothers. Their sisters. Their daughters. Within the circle of women in this community, the stages of life are honored and celebrated. The childhood of maidens here is sacred. Surrounded by women of stature and wisdom, girls and young women have role models of all ages and sizes to emulate. Girls are free to test the abilities and strengths of their minds and bodies, free to play and discover the world around them without the shadow of sexual objectification or discrimination. At the knee of their mothers, they witness the harmonious rhythm between woman and nature, and grow to respect and trust their own bodies' potential. At the onset of puberty, the maiden's passage into womanhood is celebrated by her tribe. Pregnancy is honored during a blessing ceremony that affirms the community's commitment to supporting each woman not only during pregnancy and birth, but throughout her journey as a mother. Women here are allowed to trust birth, and trust their bodies. They birth among women; worthy guides with a reverence for the birth experience in and of itself. The sisterhood of women mothers each new mother by caring for her physically and emotionally in the days and weeks after each child is born. Babies are breastfed without hesitation, each mother confident in her body's ability to create the perfect nourishment for her child; comfortable after seeing countless women in her community do the same. Women who do not birth children are valued and supported for their creative contributions to the community as well, valued for the innovation and mentorship they provide. As the mothering years pass and the children begin to have their own children, grandmothers are honored and respected as wise women. Their counsel is sought and their knowledge of the healing arts is revered. These wise women are indispensable members of the community, having lived through the challenges and experiences of a lifetime. In this time and place, the Earth is honored as Mother, and she provides clean air, clean water and an abundance of food sources as a matter of course.

As you breathe in deeply, you sense in every cell of your body that this once and future place is not only real, it is familiar to you. You know deep within your spirit that you have come home.

Take a moment now to integrate all that you see and feel; absorb this energy and let it settle into the very core of yourself. Know this is a place you can return to again and again, free to explore at your own pace, in your own time. With a last deep breath in, I invite you to slowly return to your physical body here in this space and time. With ease and grace you return to the here and now, feeling the shift of what you now know. Welcome back!

FOR DEEPER REFLECTION

What cultural messages have you internalized about the cultural experience of women?

In what ways are you currently preventing yourself from connecting with the Sacred Feminine?

What would it feel like to give yourself permission to imagine and manifest a different reality for girls and women?

THE TAPROOT

n a monotheistic God-centric world, it can be next to impossible for women to develop a regular practice of connecting with the Divine. Patriarchal religious dogma separates us as humans from Source, and systematically shames and blames us as women for all that is evil in the world. We are told at every turn that we are not worthy, we are inherently less than; we are nothing more than errant chattel for man's mission of domination and procreation. Denied the opportunity to see ourselves as the worthy and holy incarnations of the Beloved, our spirits often wither and atrophy from malnourishment. But with an intentional practice of personally identifying and connecting with Source, we tap into the wild and wise Sacred Feminine power that is within each of us, and offer ourselves much-needed spiritual nourishment.

MEDITATION

Close your eyes and take a deep breath in, and as you exhale, imagine yourself in the womb. Perfectly formed, perfectly nurtured. Every physical need met, you are surrounded by the Sacred Feminine in both body and spirit. You are connected to the Great Mother both literally and figuratively.

You spend your entire life in the womb, complete and

whole; generations of ancient women's wisdom deeply embodied in your cells and psyche.

As you grow in the womb of the Great Mother, your spirit grows too. First a beautiful seed at your conception, your spirit is now a strong sapling, shooting up into the world, and rooting down through to the Sacred Well of Gaia – the source of all spiritual replenishment.

And then you are born.

You don't know it yet, but instantly you are "less than." You are the weaker sex. The first to sin.

It takes a few years – and during those years, your little spirit sapling is growing into a lovely young tree – but eventually you start to notice:

People tell you that you can't do something because you're a girl.

You are taught to deny/repress/ignore your feelings and to be "good."

You are taught to disregard your boundaries.

You are taught to deny your intuition.

You are taught that the Goddess is a mere myth, but that God is Truth. And God is a man.

You are taught that man was created in God's image.

You are taught that women were an afterthought, and that a woman ruined everything.

You are taught that your value is directly related to your ability to attract and please men.

You are taught that enjoying and expressing your sexuality for yourself makes you a whore.

You are taught that your monthly cycle is a disgusting, dirty, inconvenient, shameful curse.

You are taught that you can't trust your body.

You are taught that wise woman traditions passed down for generations are evil and wrong.

You are taught that your identity is based on your relationship to men and children.

You are taught that you cannot possibly be trusted to give birth.

You are taught that you are not enough, and you never will be.

You are taught that, on a deep and fundamental level, you don't deserve love, and respect, and honor.

You are taught that, on a deep and fundamental level, anything female does not deserve love, respect, and honor.

And with each one of those teachings, a branch is snipped from your spirit tree. And as your branches dwindle in number, your roots atrophy, and lose their capacity to reach to the Sacred Well.

Over time, you are nearly detached from your Source, less and less able to connect to the nurturing that is your birthright. You experience this detachment as a vague sense of uncertainty, of having lost something – but not really being able to identify what it is you've lost.

But you catch clues every now and then; you have brief moments of transcendent joy. You have euphoric experiences that leave you feeling nourished deep down into your soul.

These glimpses, these moments happen because, despite the loss of so many, many limbs, one thing still remains intact in your spirit tree: your taproot.

Born female, you have an unbreakable link to the Sacred Feminine source. The taproot is the gentle voice reminding us to draw from the Sacred Well. Whether maiden, mother, or crone, the taproot is an integral part of your spiritual identity and well-being. Like a compass pointing to your true north, it helps to reveal your way to experience deep nourishment and fulfillment; it provides the spark of inspiration that compels you to create, to express, to connect.

Whatever your means of reaching deeply into the Sacred Well, you cannot fail to notice the feeling you get. You feel connected. You feel rightness. You feel like you can breathe; you can be yourself. Time seems to stand still. You feel light... unburdened. Tapped in. *Tapped in.*

And then you start to recognize the feeling when it happens, and you start to realize that those moments don't just have to happen to you: you can seek them! You start to realize, when I do ...., I feel this way! When I ...., I am one with Source.

And so you do more of that thing, of those things, and your spirit tree reacts in a magical way: it begins to grow branches again. Just a few at first, tentatively, but then more, and more – reaching up and gathering sunlight, sending nourishment down to your root system so that they can grow too. It becomes a positive-feedback loop; as more roots reach the Sacred Well and nourish the connection, more limbs and leaves can grow, which in turn allows for the roots to flourish.

This healthy cycle of nourishment and inspiration is medicine not only for your own soul, but for those around you, and for the world. And as you heal yourself by reconnecting to the Sacred Well, you begin to grow not only branches and leaves, but seeds as well. (These might be fruit, or pinecones, or nuts – depending on what type of tree you are!) These seeds are the gift that you give to the world, your contribution back to the Sacred Well. Providing inspiration and nourishment to other women, your seeds help to ensure the survival of the Sacred Feminine and the shifting of the greater global consciousness.

With another deep inhale and exhale, take a moment to remember this feeling of complete awareness of your taproot, and the Source. Offer yourself gratitude for your commitment to your well-being, knowing you can return here at any time. With ease, shift your focus now to your body, bringing awareness to the here and now. When you are ready, open your eyes. Welcome back!

FOR DEEPER REFLECTION

What cultural messages have you internalized about your ability to commune with the Divine?

In what ways are you currently preventing yourself from directly experiencing oneness with Source?

What would it feel like to give yourself permission to tap into the Sacred Feminine?

I'M NOT SORRY

s women, the apology reflex is deeply ingrained from an early age. Many of us don't realize how frequently we say "sorry" during the course of the average day, and it is indeed a profound awakening when we become aware of how thoroughly conditioned we are to apologize for simply being female, for existing. By inviting an intentional practice of offering apologies only when they are warranted, we give ourselves permission to take up space, and cultivate alignment with our authentic Sacred Feminine truth.

MEDITATION

Take a deep breath, close your eyes and allow yourself to sink into complete relaxation. Follow your breath, and with your inner vision, begin to notice that it is twilight in a beautiful forest. The golden light of evening is sparkling through the leaves of the ancient woods, and the path ahead is well-worn and welcoming. You walk with ease among the trees, feeling beautifully held by the creek on one side of your path, and the exposed rock ledges of a small ridge on the other side.

After walking for some time and taking in all of the sights and sounds, you notice the mouth of a cave within the rock ledge, and you approach it with curiosity.

You smell the damp earth of the cave and feel the cool air within as you step under the ledge. As you move further into the space, you notice with a start that there is an older woman in the cave, sitting on the earth and tending a small flame.

"Oh! I'm sorry!" you say reflexively. "I didn't know there was anyone in here."

With the flame casting just enough light to make out her features, you notice everything about this woman, and sense her deep wisdom. As your eyes adjust, you also notice that the walls of the cave are covered in innumerable tally marks, as though someone were keeping track of a great number of – *something*.

The wise old woman smiles warmly and gestures for you to sit near the flame with her, and says, "Join me."

"Oh – no, I'm sorry. I should leave you to your fire."

At these words, the wise woman picks up a piece of stone and etches two more tally marks into the cave wall.

"What are you counting?" you ask.

"Apologies," she replies. "The walls of this cave are covered with the record of how many times you have said 'I'm sorry' when an apology was not warranted or necessary."

You take in her words but feel unsure of what she means, and say, "Sorry… but I don't really understand what you're saying."

She etches another tally mark into the wall.

"Sister," she says, "all your life, you have been conditioned to believe that you are required to apologize – for everything! Your default response to everything from taking up space, to knowing your truth, to having boundaries, to feeling your feelings is to say 'I'm sorry.' You were programmed from the beginning to diminish yourself by apologizing, to keep yourself small with contrition."

Letting her words sink deep into your spirit, you feel the profound truth she has revealed. You see the tally marks on the walls and think back on the many times when saying 'I'm sorry' was an automatic response, knowing the words came from your lips without a conscious thought because it was so deeply ingrained in you.

"Yes," you say. "This is how we are taught to approach the world! To apologize for thinking, for feeling, for speaking, for *being*."

"Indeed it is," says the wise woman. "And with every needless apology, a permanent mark is left on your spirit. After a time, the marks begin to shape who you think you are. The words begin to shape your perception of yourself. You don't just say the words: you *believe* them. You believe that you are an imposition, and less deserving."

You nod in agreement.

"But this is not who you truly are. It is nothing more than a script you were handed at birth because you were born female. It is nothing more than lines you were taught to repeat on cue. You are so much more than this."

"But shouldn't I say 'I'm sorry' sometimes though?" you ask. "What if I hurt my friend's feelings or accidentally step on my daughter's foot? It would be kind of rude not to apologize, wouldn't it?"

The wise woman replies, "It is one thing to offer a sincere apology when you have made a mistake or wronged someone; taking responsibility for your actions is the path to power. But it's another thing entirely to say 'I'm sorry' a hundred times a day because you have the audacity to exist. You relinquish your power when you abide by that script."

"Yes, you're right," you say. "I never realized how constrained and controlled I felt by that!"

The wise woman replies, "And now that you know, you can never go back to not knowing. You have seen through the illusion of your culture, and can release yourself from that pattern. You have permission to stop saying I'm sorry for things that do not require an apology."

"Yes, I do. I give myself permission to burn the script. Without apology."

With a smile and a nod, the old woman validates your sovereignty and wisdom.

You take one last look around the cave at the tally marks on the walls.

"No more," you say. "No more needless apologies. No more diminishing myself or disconnecting from my authenticity and power. I'm *not* sorry for speaking my truth, or feeling my feelings, or taking up space!"

The wise woman rises from her seat on the floor and walks with you back to the mouth of the cave. With a warm embrace, you internalize her wisdom and blessing and offer your deep gratitude. She kisses you on the cheek and waves goodbye as you begin your journey back up the path. Walking through the forest, you stand taller and your stride demonstrates your confidence and clarity. You make a commitment to yourself to maintain awareness about how and when you offer apologies.

Shifting your awareness now back into this moment, you notice how you feel, both physically and emotionally. Returning to your body with ease and grace as you are ready, you take another deep breath in and exhale. Welcome back!

FOR DEEPER REFLECTION

What cultural messages have you internalized regarding the expectation and habit of apologizing?

In what ways are you currently diminishing yourself with unnecessary apologies?

What would it feel like to give yourself permission to stop saying "I'm sorry" for things that do not require an apology?

THE POWER OF NO

"No" is not a word we women are invited to own and use with authority. So conditioned are we to be pleasing and accommodating that we often forget that "no" is an option. Consequently, our most precious resources – our attention, our time, and our energy – are depleted as certainly as sands falling through an hourglass. Our well-being suffers as a result, and though we can often readily identify our feelings of being physically and emotionally exhausted, it can be difficult to make the initial connection between our ability to exercise our sovereignty and our overall spiritual health. When we tap into the wild and wise power of no, we give ourselves permission to selectively channel our Sacred Feminine resources, and to cultivate well-being and healing.

MEDITATION

Take a deep breath in, and as you exhale, take a moment to clear your mind of any thoughts right now. Just feel your body rooted down on the ground, feel your heart beating... follow your breath in and out for a cycle or two.

I invite you to imagine with me that it is morning. Tomorrow morning, let's say. And tomorrow morning, as with each new day, you have access to a *limited* amount of time and energy and resources; this is just the law of life. But as we all know, each new day brings us what seems like an unlimited number of demands, expectations, interactions, reactions, plans, needs, and wants... and with each of these, we are given the opportunity to align with our most authentic selves... by utilizing the power of "no."

One of life's most fundamental truths is that when we say *yes* to one thing, we are always, *inherently*, saying *no* to something else.

When we say yes to fear, we are saying no to love.

When we say yes to resentment, we are saying no to connection.

When we say yes to self-loathing, we are saying no to empowerment.

When we say yes to manipulation, we are saying no to our inherent sovereignty.

When we say yes to body shame, we are saying no to our sacredness.

And just as it is the law of life that each time we say yes to one thing, we say no to something else, it is also true that when we say no to something, we say yes to something else.

When we say no to guilt, we say yes to liberation.

When we say no to self-doubt, we say yes to passion.

When we say no to cultural brainwashing, we say yes to self-love and acceptance.

When we say no to being a victim, we say yes to self-worth.

When we say no to participating in unhealthy relationships, we say yes to a healthy relationship with our selves.

When we say no to martyrdom, we say yes to self-care.

When we say no to our "shoulds," we say yes to our potential.

When we say no to perfectionism, we say yes to the beauty of synchronicity.

When we say no to anxiety, we say yes to our power to manifest.

When we say no to laying blame, we say yes to accountability.

Every day, we experience countless opportunities to choose *yes*, or choose *no*.

Each moment, each interaction with others, each conversation we have with ourselves in our head is a pivotal chance to align with our sacred self, our authentic truth, and *choose*.

You have the power, in every single moment, to ask yourself what may be the most important question you will ever answer: what will I invest my precious time and energy in *right now*? What will I say no to, so that I may allow space to say yes to what really matters?

And now I invite you to participate in a writing meditation with me. On one page of your journal, you will write words. These words are seeds for exploring *your* power of no. So in this moment, you'll simply write the following words:

faith	addiction
trust	pleasure
honoring myself	sexuality
joyful movement	exhaustion
nourishing my	restriction
physical body	abundance

And I now invite you to add three or four seed words of your own to this list.

And when you are ready, take these seed words and place them in the following phrase:

When I say no to .... ,

I am saying yes to ....

Reflecting now on the deep wisdom that you have just tapped into, offer yourself a moment of gratitude, and set an intention to cultivate a practice around this new awareness. When you are ready, begin to shift your focus back to your body in this present moment. With a final deep inhale and exhale, welcome yourself back.

FOR DEEPER REFLECTION

What cultural messages have you internalized about saying no?

In what ways are you currently preventing yourself from claiming the power of no?

What would it feel like to give yourself permission to make space for what you do want by saying no to what you do *not* want?

UNLEARNING

Much like the programming of a computer, our experience as western women of the twenty-first century is very much encoded in our society: from our language, to our government, to our jobs, the cultural hierarchy that perpetuates the usurping of women's power is ubiquitous – so much so that we often cannot see the forest for the trees. We have been assimilated by patriarchy to the point that we may not know where it ends and we begin. By awakening to the wild and wise process of unlearning, we relinquish the power of patriarchy to define our value, and reclaim our ability to connect with our innate Sacred Feminine power.

MEDITATION

Take a deep breath in, and exhale fully, inviting relaxation into every cell of your body. Feel yourself held and supported, knowing that this journey is safe and that you are supported by the sisterhood of women who have walked this path ahead of you.

Like you, we have heard the call of the Sacred Feminine, and our spirits have responded to that call with an undeniable 'Yes!' But the path isn't without obstacles, and we sometimes feel disconnected from our divinity despite our deep longing for evolution. Instead of hearing the affirmations of our sacred selves, we still hear the negative feedback loop that many of us have heard for as long as we can remember.

I invite you now to take a moment to write down some of those negative messages that you hear – messages that are so deeply learned that they feel like they are a part of you.

These are the messages that start with:

"I cannot…"

"I do not know how to…"

"I am not…"

"I should not…"

Once you have written down as many as you can think of, place them in front of you, and settle in with closed eyes once again.

And we'll begin our journey, back, connecting to the time before you learned that your whole person was being judged based on your physical appearance. Back before you were told that you can't trust your body or your instincts. Before you learned that your value as a person is based on being sexually attractive to men. Go back, before you learned that bleeding is shameful and dirty. Before you learned that "being good" means not speaking your truth or having healthy boundaries. Before you learned to disconnect from the fact that you have a monthly cycle. Before you learned that other women are the enemy. Before you were taught that you are not enough, and never will be. Before you were taught that you are failing as a mother – and failing as a woman if you are not a mother.

Back before this time of the *shamed* feminine, there was the era of the Sacred Feminine. It was a time of women's wisdom, and women's power. We were holy; we were whole. Women were taught by their mothers, and their mother's mothers, to stand in their power, and they were neither controlled nor dominated. Women passed their wisdom down to one-another, and lived cooperatively rather than competitively, and quite naturally had an equal voice in what happened in their world.

But gradually, between then and now, there was a great shift; a cultural re-write took place. Instead of being revered, women were taught that they were inherently flawed. Women's bodies, once honored, were instead said to be incapable, and the gift of their life-giving cycle became a curse. Women learned to hide it, to stop it, to fear it. Even birth was something women could no longer be trusted to do without male oversight.

Women's connection to the Divine, once a source of deep meaning and power, became evil and taboo. The wise women were discredited as hysterical lunatics, as wild witches. Those who tried to keep their wisdom alive were burned at the stake.

Women heard songs of their domination, and stories were told from the time they were babies to teach them that their only hope for salvation, of true happiness, was the love and approval of a man. The messages were inescapable; so much so that the women internalized them. And when they became mothers, they taught their daughters this as their own truth. The books were scrubbed clean of stories of their ancestors' power, of the wisdom that is their birthright; and what was taught forever more was called *his*tory!

And now, with so much time having passed, we no longer question what we are expected to learn. We don't even *know* what we don't know.

But there is a part of us: the thread that still connects us to the wise women of our lineage – and *she* still knows.

To find her, simply look at what you wrote down and ask yourself:

Are these my truths? Or just the script I was expected to learn during this life?

Are these my mother's truths, and her mother's truths? Or are these nothing more than the programming that the women in my motherline learned to believe?

Opening your eyes now, I invite you to begin the process of unlearning by taking your pen and striking through all of the negative messages you have learned and internalized about yourself. If you have written "I should not," mark out the "not," and read your new statement aloud. If you have written "I am not," cross out the "not" and affirm this new message to yourself. Continue this process until you have reprogrammed your internal dialogue.

When you have finished, place your journal and pen aside and with another deep inhale and exhale, close your eyes once more.

The strength, the wisdom, the reverence for the Sacred Feminine was at one time ours to claim, during the time before the beyond. And with your revolutionary act of unlearning, you reclaim this once again, in the here and now. Reaching within, connecting to the brilliantly radiant Sacred Feminine seed that we ALL possess, we can affirm for *ourselves* the gifts of our lineage: self-worth, reverence, sisterhood, wisdom and strength.

With a last inhale, offer yourself deep gratitude for initiating this practice of unlearning, and commit to the process of reprogramming your inner language, starting now. Gently, begin to shift your awareness to your body, back to this present moment. Move slowly and with ease as you return to here and now. When you are ready, open your eyes. Welcome back!

FOR DEEPER REFLECTION

What cultural messages have you internalized about what it means to be a woman?

In what ways are you currently preventing yourself from aligning with your truth?

What would it feel like to give yourself permission to rewrite your inner narrative?

WOMB ROOM

ow many of us are told as girls and young women that our body is sacred, and that indeed our womb-space, our pelvic bowl, is the seat of our power? Divorced as we are from our bodies and our Sacred Feminine core, it is difficult for us to find a holy and whole sanctuary within ourselves; it is difficult for us to identify or find the locus of our innate wisdom and strength. And yet, it is there, in all of us, waiting for our discovery. For those of us with a history of sexual trauma or abuse, and even for those of us whose sexual trauma is the result of simply living in this culture, the journey to our Womb Room may be fraught with obstacles. But with a devoted practice of discovery, we can find it. We can heal it… and it can heal us. Whatever our personal history, connecting with the wild and wise presence of our Womb Room is a life-changing experience in communing with the deepest and most fundamental aspect of our Sacred Feminine selves.

MEDITATION

Take a deep breath in, and as you exhale, allow yourself to relax fully, melting down into the support of the earth below you. Follow your breath… feel your heart beating her rhythm. You connect with this rhythm, and begin to become aware that this is the sound of footsteps on a path… not only your own, but the footsteps of your three guides, walking along ahead of you, each bearing a torch.

You note the appearance of the first: a young woman, with a white dress tied with a red sash around her waist. You recognize her as The Maiden. Behind her, you see a stunning woman, radiant and full-bellied in late pregnancy. You recognize her as The Mother. And next, between yourself and The Mother, you see a woman with long silver hair, and a walking staff in one hand. You recognize The Crone.

Following with ease and grace, you have complete faith in your guides – although you do not know where you are, nor do you know your destination. Walking in silence, you take time to notice your surroundings, thankful for the magical light of a beautiful full moon.

From time to time, one of your three guides glances back to offer a reassuring smile, and your curiosity finally gets the better of you.

"Where are you taking me, dear guides?"

The Crone turns around with a knowing smile, and winks at you.

"All will be revealed in time, my love," she says.

You walk further on, aware of all that surrounds you, now with even more anticipation.

Finally… you arrive.

"Welcome," says The Maiden, "to the very seat of your Sacred Feminine spirit. This is the realm of your female identity, the home of your beliefs about being female and all that you embody and personify. This is where your Womb Room resides."

"But what is my Womb Room?" you ask.

"See for yourself…" says The Mother, and she hands you her torch. She gestures beyond your path, and you see it – your Womb Room.

"Now is the time for you to shine the light of Wisdom and Love into your Womb Room," says The Crone.

"We have created this time and space of complete safety for you to explore every inch, every corner, every shadow. Take this torch and continue on without us. This is *your* journey now," says The Maiden.

"We will be holding space for you, and will call you back when the time comes," says The Crone.

"When you hear three chimes – one for The Maiden, one for The Mother, and one for The Crone – you will know it is time to return to us here on the trail."

You take the torch from The Maiden, and step away from your guides, walking in the direction of your Womb Room.

Illuminated by the full moon's radiance, you see it at last. You stop and pause to notice all of the details of the exterior, and as you walk around to explore from all sides, you see that there is an entrance leading inside. Trusting The Maiden, The Mother, and The Crone to surround you with safety and love, you enter your Womb Room.

After stepping across the threshold, you pause, taking in all that you see. The radiance of the full moon seems magnified in this space, and you have the perfect amount of light to notice all of the details of your surroundings. Feeling completely safe, you step in and begin exploring… in your own time, at your own pace, trusting your inner voice to guide you in this journey.

(((*Wait 4-5 minutes; ring chime three times*)))

Hearing the chime of your Guides, you take one last look around you, absorbing all that you have seen. You step out of your Womb Room and begin to make your way back to the waiting women on the trail.

As you rejoin them, they greet you with welcoming smiles and loving eyes.

"What beautiful work you have done, sister. We honor your journey," says The Maiden.

"What questions do you have for us, beloved?" asks The Mother.

You ask any questions that are weighing upon your heart, and are answered with the exact words you need to hear.

The Crone bows to you and says, "Wise Woman, it is now time for our return."

Gesturing ahead, The Crone waits for you to take the lead, and she steps in behind you as you begin your walk back up the trail. Following behind The Crone, you hear the steps of The Mother and The Maiden, and know that you are worthy of this company.

Using the moonlight and your intuition to guide you, you make your way back... up and up... finding your way back to your body. Here in this space and time, once again. Welcome back!

FOR DEEPER REFLECTION

What cultural messages have you internalized about your womb space/uterus?

In what ways are you currently preventing yourself from connecting to your Sacred Feminine core?

What would it feel like to give yourself permission to regularly explore and inhabit your Womb Room?

HUNGER

h, how we are taught to hate our hunger! To deny it, to repress it, to make it our enemy. In a world of material abundance, we learn that we are most valuable and worthy when we win the war against our cravings and normalize the doctrine of denial. Compelled to comply with this codex and silence our yearnings, we grow into women who can no longer feel what it is we are hungry for. We don't know what our body needs; we don't know what our spirit craves. When we cultivate an intentional practice of hearing and heeding our wild and wise hunger, we give ourselves permission to return to wholeness, to find fulfillment and pleasure in the nourishment of our bodies and souls. When we recognize our hunger as holy, we allow ourselves to feed the Sacred Feminine spirit within.

MEDITATION

Take a deep breath in and exhale, allowing your body to sink down into the floor. Inhale once again and allow the breath to fill your body from crown to toes. Rest your hands just above your belly button, finding the place on your physical body where you first notice when you are hungry.

Tune into this area. Tap into the sensation of hunger, even if it's only a memory... and imagine what it would be like to give yourself permission to fully nourish that hunger. What kinds of foods would you feed yourself? Allow yourself to exist for just a moment in this liminal space, free of any judgment or cultural shame you hold around food. Imagine the food that you most deeply crave… and imagine eating it! Notice your feelings of nourishment, acceptance, and love.

And as you observe your feelings, you become aware that even after having fed your body in response to your physical hunger, you may feel *full*, but you still do not feel sated. With curiosity and openness, you shift one hand to your heart, and realize the hunger you feel is not centered in your body, but rooted in your heart. Connecting to her rhythm, you begin to hear the whisperings of her desire. You listen, and she speaks to you of her hunger. In words and images and feelings, your heart beats the steady pulse of what would most nourish her.

Breathing in and truly awakening to this message, you now move your other hand to your solar plexus, at the center point of your ribs, just below your breasts. At this very root of your ability to say "I want," your solar plexus connects you to your deepest hunger – the hunger of your soul. Attuned now to this sensation, you are able to easily hear and see what your soul is starving for. The message is undeniable; you *feel* it in your body as an ache that you can no longer *not* be aware of. What does your spirit most need to be fed right now? You now possess the knowledge of what would most nourish and nurture the hunger in your soul.

And with this knowledge, you are now able to begin to imagine exactly how to feed your heart and your spirit. Imagine what it would be like to give yourself permission to fully nourish that hunger. How would you feed yourself? Imagine feeding your heart and soul what they most deeply crave...

Connecting with pure grace and ease on this spirit level with yourself, you may now take a moment to fully grant yourself permission to hear and respond to your hunger – the hunger of your body, your heart, and your soul. Acknowledge each craving, and if you wish, make a commitment to yourself to begin to feed this hunger, knowing that your hunger provides valuable insight into your own well-being. Knowing that though you may have lacked nurturing from others in your life, you are fully equipped and capable of nurturing yourself. Knowing that you are without a doubt so very worthy and deserving of being fed.

With both hands over your heart now, take a moment to receive the gratitude offered by your body, heart, and soul – gratitude for your willingness to hear and see and feel their hunger. Gratitude for your commitment to nourish and feed your self. With a deep breath in, begin to move your body, bringing yourself slowly back to this moment. Welcome back!

FOR DEEPER REFLECTION

What cultural messages have you internalized about hunger?

In what ways are you currently preventing yourself from aligning with your yearnings?

What would it feel like to give yourself permission to cultivate a practice of honoring your cravings?

TENDING YOUR BODY TEMPLE

Our female bodies: our messy, fragile, complex, power-ful, wise female bodies. Is there an entity on Earth with whom we have a more complicated relation-ship? From our first breath to our last, our physical body is our constant companion: the temple of our soul. And yet how much intentional awareness do we offer this miracle of creation, this marvel of biological engineering? How often do we silence our harsh inner critic and simply tune in, truly, and deeply listen to the messages that our body is offering? When we cultivate appreciative awareness of our wild and wise temples, we offer ourselves the opportunity to integrate our body and soul: to know ourselves as whole. When we give ourselves permission to lovingly connect with each and every part of our physical selves, we invite the healing of our Sacred Feminine spirit.

MEDITATION

Take a deep breath in, and as you exhale, allow your consciousness to feel very light... so light that you find your awareness floating up and out of your physical body. Inhale and rise up... exhale and settle into this space, hovering just above your body, seeing yourself here in just as you are.

Without judgment, observe your physical body from this vantage point. Take a moment now to see yourself as you would gaze upon a beloved friend, or as a mother would see her daughter. Feel in your heart the unconditional love and gratitude and blessings for all that your body does for you. Even if your body struggles to achieve optimal health, she got you here today. She is trying. Give your disembodied consciousness permission to express this love in whatever way she feels called.

Lightly floating up to your resting space again, I invite you now to notice your skin... the largest organ of our body, our skin creates the boundary between our *self* and the rest of the world. Our skin protects and contains us, and absorbs all that is around us – for better or for worse. Everything that touches our skin becomes a part of us: lotions, creams, shampoos, perfume, deodorant – all absorbed diligently by our skin into our bloodstream. We can nourish our skin from within and without by choosing purified water, and care products that nurture rather than harm us. Take a moment now and tune in with your physical body – with your skin. Ask your skin what she wants and needs... and listen to her reply. Thank your skin for her devotion to you.

I invite you now to shift your consciousness to your muscles and bones and joints – the parts of you that move you. Our bodies were built to move; in days past, movement meant survival. And now, with this sedentary twenty-first century lifestyle, many of us have lost the joy of movement. We have become disconnected from our innate power and strength, and from the spirituality of moving for pure pleasure.

Tune in with your bones and muscles now, and ask your musculoskeletal system what she wants and needs.

What movement does your body crave? What physical practice would nourish and strengthen you? Thank your muscles and bones for their devotion to you.

And now we will shift our awareness to our cardio-vascular and respiratory systems – our heart, lungs, and blood. The home of our breath and seat of our emotional body, our lungs and heart work without rest to fuel our bodies with oxygen and nourishment for all of the work and play and passion that we choose. Ready in an instant, our cardiovascular and respiratory systems are on stand-by 24/7 to serve us. I invite you now to tune in with your heart, and lungs, and blood… and ask them what they want and need. Feel the rhythm and the pulse of your body, and thank your heart and blood and lungs for their devotion to you.

I invite you now to shift your awareness to your diges-tive system – your stomach and intestines.

Tasked with sorting through all that we ingest, and separating the nourishing from the unusable, our diges-tive system does its darndest to keep our cells fueled and functional. But what a terrible time to be a digestive system! Like the king demanding that Rumplestiltskin spin straw into gold, we often expect our stomach and intestines to perform near-magical alchemy with the onslaught of non-foods and GMOs and toxins we regularly consume. And she tries! She really tries. Take a moment now to tune in with your digestive system. Gently, kindly, ask your digestive system what would nurture and nourish her, and listen for the answer. Thank your digestive system for her devotion to you.

And lastly, I invite you to shift your awareness to your nervous system – your brain and nerves. The control center of your physical body, your nervous system makes the commands and sends them out while simultaneously integrating the incoming data stream from all of your five senses while also thinking thoughts and dreaming dreams and analyzing information without you being consciously aware of it all happening! Quite a feat! Many of us live in such a way that stimulates our nervous system to constantly be on high alert, readying our body for fight or flight as we confront such threats to our very survival as to-do lists, traffic, deadlines, finances, children, spouses, ex-spouses, and saber-toothed tigers. Rarely given time to de-escalate from DEFCON 5, our nervous system can be prone to short-circuiting and misappropriating, but only because she tries so hard to keep us alive. Breathing in now a sense of well-being and calm, I invite you to tune in with your nervous system and ask her what she most needs and wants. What would calm and nourish her? Listen for the answer. Thank your nervous system for her devotion to you.

With a deep breath in, I invite you now to gently rejoin your physical self... reintegrate your consciousness and your body. Feel the weight of your hands and legs being supported by the floor. Feel the rhythm of your heart, and the cycling of your breath.

For many of us, there is a tendency toward having a love-hate, or even a hate-hate, relationship with our bodies, focusing on all of the things that we dislike or wish were different. But as with other relationships in our life, we have the choice to cultivate kindness, compassion, and gratitude for our bodies. We all struggle to remain devoted stewards of our body temples, but as Rob Brezny reminds us:

"Thousands of things go right for you every day, beginning the moment you wake up."

It is an act of radical revolution to *unlearn* the habits of self-hate, punishment, withholding, abuse, and criticism, instead choosing to accept and cherish and nurture our body temples, to inventory all that goes right every day, to create a practice of asking and listening to our bodies, and to give ourselves permission to say *yes* to what our bodies want and need.

With a final deep inhale, begin to shift your awareness back to this present moment, inviting gentle movement and, when you are ready, opening your eyes. Welcome back!

FOR DEEPER REFLECTION

What cultural messages have you internalized about your body?

In what ways are you currently preventing yourself from cultivating a positive relationship with your body?

What would it feel like to give yourself permission to regularly honor and tend to your body?

ALL OF YOU

How many of **you** are there? We may live under the illusion that we are the one that we see in the mirror every day, and nothing more. But look deeper within and you will find your interior multiverse populated with an assemblage of your many identities: the Daughter, the Lover, the Warrior, the Mother – each with something important to say. When we cultivate a practice of inviting our wild and wise inner identities to communicate, we open the door to profound insight and self-awareness. When we commit to compassionately seeing and hearing each and every part of ourselves, our integration perpetuates healing, and our Sacred Feminine spirit is once again whole.

MEDITATION

Take a deep breath in and invite your body to relax fully. Pause and follow your breath for a few cycles, sensing your unique inner rhythm. As you hear your heart beat, imagine you hear the sound of your own footsteps on a path… a path within the most beautiful and sacred environment you can imagine. This may be an ancient redwood forest, a pristine beach, a mountain-top meadow, or anywhere your spirit feels most safe, nourished and at peace. In this sacred space, you see a circle which you realize is intended for a gathering of many women.

You feel called and welcomed into this space, and find your way to the spot that feels most comfortable to you. Sink into this space with ease, knowing that all is just as it should be.

After a few moments of enjoying this blissful solitude, you hear footsteps approaching on the path. You look up to see not just someone else walking toward you, but another *you* stepping toward the circle. But it's not *you* exactly... it's one facet of you, one of the myriad identities you have embodied throughout your lifetime. She may be The Artist or The Mother. She may be The Daughter or The Survivor. Ask her now to reveal her identity to you, and listen to what she says. Speaking her name or title back to her, welcome this part of your Self to your sacred circle.

As the next few moments pass, you see one *you* after another walking along the path toward your circle. As with the first, you greet each aspect of yourself and welcome her into your sacred gathering space. When you sense that all of your Selves are present in the Circle, you speak...

"My Beloved Selves," you say, "you honor me by stepping forth and revealing yourselves to me in this sacred space. I know that you have all been integral in my evolution as a woman, and for that I hold deep gratitude. I also know that some of you may have shouldered an unfair burden throughout my journey, and many of you have become almost completely disconnected and cut off from any spiritual nourishment. Because of this, I know that I am an incomplete expression of my most authentic Self. We gather here in this sacred space today so that I may re-member all of you. Re. Member. Reconnect. Nourish. And integrate all of my Selves into the Whole."

You feel the love pulsing from each of your Selves, grateful for the opportunity to be seen and heard in this sacred manner.

You ask your Selves who would like to step forward first for the Re-Membering ritual, and you watch who comes forth. You call her by her name or title once again, and you ask her what it is she needs in order to heal, grow, and integrate into the Whole You. She voices her needs... and you not only hear, but feel her words. You look into her eyes, and feel your soul connect completely with this facet of yourself. With divine love, you say, "I see you, I hear you, I feel you, I honor you, My Sacred Self." In unison, all of the other Selves in the circle whisper, "So may it be."

Your Self holds her hands over her heart, receiving this blessing with deep gratitude. And then with one step forward, she steps *into* your body, merging with you in psyche and spirit.

You then call forth the next aspect of your Self, and ask her what she needs in order to heal, grow, and integrate into the Whole You. She voices her needs, and you and the other Selves in your circle hear and bless her.

And so the ritual repeats... until all of your Selves have been seen and heard and integrated. With ease and grace, your Spirit welcomes – re-members – all of you.

You take a moment now, in this still quiet of your sacred space, and sense this new wholeness of your Self. Absorb and embody all that your separate Selves shared with you, all that they asked for. Take a moment to honor your Self, and your Selves, and to make a commitment to yourself in this moment, knowing that this peace and grace is available to you any time you should need it. Knowing you have the strength and wisdom to make this journey again, to commune with all of you, anytime you should need to. And with a final blessing of love to your Self and your Selves, you rise and begin your gentle walk back up the path, returning with ease to this space and time, here and now. Welcome back!

FOR DEEPER REFLECTION

What cultural messages have you internalized about your sense of self?

In what ways are you currently preventing yourself from hearing and healing your wounded self/selves?

What would it feel like to give yourself permission to lovingly integrate the many aspects of your sacred self?

SERENDIPITY

The idea of serendipity – a fortunate unplanned occurrence – is one that can be found in world cultures throughout history. Call it fate, karma, luck, synchronicity or coincidence, there is a general human awareness of the responsiveness of the universe to our energetic expressions. When we actively bring awareness to the wild and wise synchronicity of the events of our life, we tap into the profound creative power of our thoughts, words, and actions. When we flow with the energetic vibration of the Sacred Feminine, we unleash our full potential to magnetize and manifest.

MEDITATION

You may not know me. Or rather, you may not *know* that you know me. But I have known you… I have walked with you, since the moment of your birth. An energetic pulse without a physical body, I am everywhere you are, always in tune with the frequency of your thoughts and emotions. Like a law of nature, I respond not because of any *desire* to do so, but because the universe is woven in such a way that it is a given. You think… you feel… you plan… you wish… you hope… you pray… I respond.

I *conspire*, you could even say. I traverse the web of time and space to deliver just what you need, just when you need it.

The book that you open – sometimes even to a specific passage on a random page – that says the words you most need to hear? It's no coincidence that the book found you when it did.

The song you hear, with words of affirmation, of hope, of breaking and then mending again. It's no coincidence the song found you when it did.

The person you meet? The one you weren't expecting, but who becomes your safety net and your rock? It's no coincidence you found each other when you did.

The job offer you get? The one that allows you to shift into even deeper alignment with yourself? It was no coincidence the job found you when it did.

The job offer you *didn't get*? The one that shifted you in a completely different direction? It was no coincidence that your path changed directions when it did.

The friend you bump into... the one you haven't seen in the longest time? The healing that came from that interaction at that moment was no coincidence.

The path that brought you here, to this exact moment. Your presence here, now, is no coincidence.

These moments, these events, are far from random... they are instead akin to the movements in a symphony; each instrument representing a decision or a relationship or an event in your life. Witnessed individually, these instruments – these moments – may seem unrelated, but when you step back and are able to perceive the entire orchestra, you begin to hear the music of your life.

And I – responding to your thoughts, your feelings, your wishes, prayers, intentions – lead the orchestra like a conductor – in most cases, without you being aware of this gentle, constant guidance.

Who am I? I am Serendipity.

Knowing now that I am here, you can reflect back on countless events in your life that were energetically orchestrated... not *by* me, but *through* me, as a result of your choices and thoughts and ideas. We, the orchestra and the conductor, merely play the music that *you* write. And such beautiful music it is, always evolving toward your highest expression of your sacred self.

With awareness of my existence, you have the ability to create even more harmony in your orchestra. With the understanding that *you* write the music, and that the orchestra and I respond, you can begin to fine-tune your own frequency, making a practice of foreseeing the reality that you wish to create, and feeling the energetic vibration around that reality.

And while I do respond to what thoughts and feelings may reside below even your own conscious awareness, the power of my ability to conduct the orchestra of your life is amplified by your *conscious* thoughts, feelings, prayers, intentions, and desires. The more aware you become of these, the more frequently you will be aware of my presence in your life. Speak your intention. Write your prayer. Chant your mantra. Give thanks for unknowing blessings on their way. These actions have power in their unique vibration, the frequency of which is the language I speak.

On this journey... as you walk your path toward your most authentic and sacred self, know that I am here. Watch for me, listen for me, feel for me. You will soon be able to see, hear, and feel me all around you, in the little things. In the big things. I am here, unfailingly. I am Serendipity.

FOR DEEPER REFLECTION

What cultural messages have you internalized about coincidence or luck?

In what ways are you currently preventing yourself from activating your power to manifest?

What would it feel like to give yourself permission to cultivate a relationship with a responsive universe?

YOUR INNER WARRIOR

Facing the world with our fiercest persona is a habit for some of us, in some cases the consequence of literally fighting for our survival, but in many cases the unfortunate result of the culture in which we live. We women spend such a high proportion of our lives in fight or flight mode that we literally exhaust our adrenals and deplete our spirits, and find ourselves running on fumes more often than not. So ingrained is this status-quo that many of us have forgotten that we can give ourselves permission to let go of our white-knuckle grip on life and that we can allow ourselves to create safe spaces in which we can surrender to stillness. When we hear and nurture the needs of our Inner Warrior, we cultivate awareness of our own inner strength. When we offer our Inner Warrior the opportunity to let down her guard, to rest and receive, we tap into the limitless healing potential of our wild and wise Sacred Feminine core.

MEDITATION

It's dark, and you and I are standing together. I offer you a source of light, and you take it in hand, knowing you will need it for your journey. You know that even though I have come this far with you, the rest of the journey must be yours alone. I hold your hand and kiss your forehead, sensing your mixed emotions... hesitation, curiosity, and resolve.

"How will I find her?" you ask.

"Use your heart," I respond. "She is waiting for you... she has always been waiting for you. Your Inner Warrior needs you now, and she knows that now is the time for you to meet face to face."

You nod in affirmation, feeling ready for this journey. You have everything you need.

I blow you a kiss, one hand over my heart, as you prepare for the journey to meet your Inner Warrior.

You breathe and take a moment to reflect on the times when your Inner Warrior has risen to protect you, to defend you, to keep you safe. All the times you have survived, either emotionally or physically, because of her.

You tune into her energy, feel her emotional vibration. You imagine where she might be.

In a flash of insight, you know where she is, and you know how to get there.

Your journey begins, and you travel with confidence to the location of your Inner Warrior.

When you arrive, she is waiting for you.

You see her, perhaps for the first time in your life, and she sees you.

"Beautiful and brave Warrior, I am here," you say.

You listen intently to what she says in return.

You then say, "You have done such an amazing job of keeping me safe, of going to battle for me. What I want you to know right now is that it is time for you to rest. You don't have to fight to survive anymore. I am here to give *you* the love you need, Warrior."

You ask her what would feel most nourishing to her; what would make her feel most loved. You listen, and then you do just what she needs. You love her in the exact way that she needs to be loved.

You then ask, "Tell me which part of you is hurting," and then listen to her response.

After she replies, you realize that you know exactly how to love her, down to the root of that hurt.

You tell her she is so worthy and deserving of love.

Next you ask, "Tell me how tired you are…" and then listen to her response.

When you hear her reply, you realize you know exactly how to love her, down to the core of her exhaustion.

You tell her she is so worthy and deserving of rest.

Finally, you ask, "Tell me how afraid you are," and then listen to her response.

When she has finished speaking, you realize you know exactly how to love her, down to the source of her fear.

You tell her she is so very safe.

You spend as much time as you need, loving and tending to your Warrior's pain and fatigue and fear. Reminding her all the while that she is safe, she is loved, and she can rest. You remind her that she has done an amazing job of helping you to survive. You thank her from the very foundation of your heart and soul.

You tell her that it is time for you to make your return, and ask her if there is anything she wishes to say or ask before you leave, and then you listen to her response.

When you respond, you know exactly what she needs to hear.

You leave your source of light there with your Warrior, knowing you are so very capable of finding your way back, and knowing that she will always be connected to your light. As you return, it is no longer dark, but warm and light with the sunrise. You see me waiting for you, one hand outstretched to greet you, one hand on my heart. Welcome back, beloved.

FOR DEEPER REFLECTION

What cultural messages have you internalized
about how you need to move through the world?

In what ways are you currently preventing
yourself from resting and releasing?

What would it feel like to give yourself
permission to let down your guard?

THE MOTHER CODE

When it comes to emotionally nurturing others – our children, our friends, our partners – we women were born for the job. Stepping into the role of mother feels quite natural in most cases, and we offer our emotional support without reservation during times of crisis. But what of ourselves? Who do we mothers turn to when we are the ones in need of stability and support? It seems that now more than ever before, we are a generation of motherless mothers, offering deep spiritual sustenance to others without receiving it ourselves. The reality is that we are all endowed with the ability to perfectly mother ourselves; the paradox is that it is sometimes the hardest thing to do when we most need it. When we consciously cultivate a practice of accessing our wild and wise Mother Code, we invite ourselves to experience nurturing in a new and profound way. When we connect with the infinite essence of our Sacred Feminine spirit, we activate the deep healing that we deserve.

MEDITATION

Take a deep breath and allow yourself to relax completely, melting into the floor. Your body feels heavy and held, as your soul lightens in preparation for travel. With your next inhale, your spirit travels easily into the space of your physical body. With ease and grace you find yourself inside of you. Allow yourself to acclimate, noticing your surroundings. With your third eye perfectly adjusted to this inner light, you see a cell – one of your cells – perfect and complete, whole unto itself. And then, something miraculous happens. You see the chromosomes begin to line up in the center of the cell: the process of mitosis has begun. You watch as the eternal creative impulse of the universe is made manifest in your very own body; as the dance of life and renewal unfolds. Within mere moments, what was one cell is now two: the mother cell, and the daughter cell. Having passed her genetic legacy to her daughter, the mother cell's work is now complete. There is no mothering. Like a hatchling turtle ready to run to the ocean and swim the moment she emerges from the egg, the daughter cell needs nothing further from her mother in order to fulfill her destiny. She too is perfect and complete; whole unto herself.

As are you, sister.

You are the daughter of your mother. But unlike a cell, we are not merely clones of our mothers, though we do hold their genetic blueprints within us. We are our mothers' daughters, complete and whole unto ourselves. And within each of our cells, we have been endowed with the universal code for mothering. And while our mothers, with their limitations of human-ness, may not have been able to mother us with the completeness that we would have liked, they gave us all something beyond their own mother-love: the ability to *mother ourselves*. We are the compass, and we are the map.

Within each and every one of our perfect cells lies the code of The Mother. And this code was passed to you from your mother, and to her from her mother, and to her from her mother. And so even if there are countless generations of daughters in your matriline who were not mothered in the way they needed, if you trace our cellular lineage back, and back further, we all arrive at the same point of origin: The Great Mother. The unfailing Mother. The Mother of Creation, the Mother of all Daughters. Her code is within us. Her code is within you.

And though we may ourselves not all be mothers, we *all* have the blueprint for mothering. Whether our impulse is to mother our own offspring, or a pet, our garden, the needy and hurt and helpless in this world, the Earth itself, or our creative projects and ideas, the legacy of mothering is indeed ours. And while we may not have been explicitly taught how to do so, we are hard-wired for the most challenging journey of all: mothering ourselves.

So imagine again the two cells: the mother and the daughter. Look closely at the daughter cell and see the chromosomes that create the blueprints for all of the possible expressions of that cell. And now look closer; look with your third eye. Within the DNA of the daughter lies the collective wisdom of the Mother Code, our legacy and birthright.

Allow yourself to feel this wisdom, this eternal vibration, in each one of your cells. Allow yourself to know that no matter what your relationship with the woman who gave birth to you, you have within you everything you need to be the perfect mother to yourself. The wisdom is yours to claim, sister. Taking time now, tuning in with the perfect vision and clarity of your spirit senses, ask the questions you have held in your heart, and allow yourself to know the answers.

With a deep inhale and exhale, you offer yourself deep love and gratitude for this new awareness, and commit to incorporating this wisdom in your healing journey. As you feel ready, you begin to shift your awareness to your body in this moment, moving with ease, and finally opening your eyes. Welcome back!

FOR DEEPER REFLECTION

What cultural messages have you internalized about being nurtured as an adult woman/ mother?

In what ways are you currently preventing yourself from prioritizing your need for nurturing?

What would it feel like to give yourself permission to honor your ability to perfectly mother yourself?

WISE WOMAN WITHIN

*H*ow many times have we sought the counsel and comfort of others, not realizing that we hold deep reserves of compassion and wisdom within ourselves? How many times have we looked outward for an answer, but feel a sense of resolution only when the answer within was revealed? The practice of cultivating a relationship with our Wise Woman Within is not something many of us are taught, but it is indeed one of the most powerfully nurturing acts of self-care we can offer ourselves. When we travel the web of time to commune with our past and future selves, we open to the immense and timeless matrix of Sacred Feminine healing.

MEDITATION

Take a deep breath and exhale completely, allowing yourself to fully relax. With another inhale, give yourself permission to leave this space and time, and travel the web of time on a strand that leads to the past... back to a moment when you were in crisis, when you most needed the support and guidance of a wise woman who could offer unconditional love. A moment when you felt alone, isolated, and unseen.

Imagine this moment with perfect clarity. You know every detail – but this time, you are seeing it through the eyes of an observer rather than the participant. You see your younger self in this moment, and feel with immediate clarity how younger you is feeling. You know what she most needs in this moment.

She sees you, and without a word, you go to her. You embrace, feeling an enormous wave of love for this beloved self of yours. Looking into your eyes, her own older, wiser eyes, she asks you why you've come... and you answer her.

In this moment, you tell her exactly what she needs to hear. You offer the understanding, the compassion, and the love that no one but you can give her. You are there for her as long as she needs you.

Before leaving, you ask your younger self if she has anything else to ask or give voice to, and she says "yes." You listen as she speaks, and then offer the response that she most needs to hear in this moment.

When you are both ready, you prepare to return to the present moment once again, and remind her that you are here for her anytime she needs you. She nods and smiles, and with one hand over your heart, you wave goodbye.

With a gentle breath, you are aware of your body once again, here in this space and time. Settle in and follow your heartbeat, sinking into your natural rhythm.

And now, bring to mind an issue or challenging situation that you are currently struggling with. Allow yourself to imagine the details of this situation; the people or places involved, and what's at stake.

With ease and grace, you now call to your future self, and ask for her presence and guidance. Instantly, she appears. You take a moment to notice everything about her, and feel a wave of admiration for the wise woman before you.

"I am here to help you, beloved," she says, and you tell her of your dilemma.

She listens carefully, and then tells you exactly what you need to hear. She offers her support without judgment, and offers love unconditionally. You feel heard and supported in a way that you have never felt before.

She asks you if there is anything else you would like to ask or give voice to. You say "yes," and she listens as you speak. She responds, and shares the wisdom you most need to hear in this moment.

You thank your future self for her guidance, and before she leaves, she reminds you that she is here for you always, anytime you need her. With a smile, she fades, and you become aware once again of your body in this space at this time. Slowly moving your body, you prepare to open your eyes. Welcome back!

FOR DEEPER REFLECTION

What cultural messages have you internalized about your ability to heal your spiritual/emotional wounds?

In what ways are you currently preventing yourself from connecting with your inner wisdom?

What would it feel like to give yourself permission to prioritize your healing?

PART II
THE INNER GODDESS

ORIGINS

The archetype of the Goddess has resonated with me profoundly since the beginning of my journey of awakening. I was introduced to this important aspect of the Sacred Feminine paradigm by a friend who regularly invoked the wisdom of *The Goddess Oracle* cards by Amy Sophia Marashinsky. Intrigued and inspired by what was reflected to me when I used the cards, I bought my own – and just like that, my life-changing journey began.

For years I studied and invoked the wisdom of the Goddess archetype and began to know myself in a way that I never had before. As I immersed myself in the ground-breaking work of Jean Shinoda Bolen, my self-knowledge became multi-dimensional, transcending time and culture; I came to understand my unique place within the legacy of my Sacred Feminine heritage. My connection with my inner wise woman, and with Spirit, was deeper and more real to me than ever before.

Years later, as I stepped into the Mother archetype when my daughter Brynn was born, I knew that her journey with the Goddess would be a fundamental and intentional aspect of her upbringing – not an accidental discovery.

When Brynn was seven years old, I was inspired to offer my first mother-daughter circle. Centered around the Sacred Feminine archetypes that had been revelatory for my personal evolution, I called the circle *Goddess Girls*. Each month, Brynn and I gathered with a group of like-minded mothers and daughters to learn about a new Goddess – but not just about her mythological or historical significance: we learned in each gathering that the Goddess was *within us*.

It was revolutionary, to say the least.

Usurping the dominant patriarchal paradigm, we were rewriting the scripts for our daughters before the cultural status-quo had the chance to take root in their psyches and souls. And an unexpected magic happened for us mothers as well; as we co-created the circle for the benefit of our daughters, we began to heal from the deep wounds of patriarchy ourselves.

Together, we addressed head-on the discomfort many women have internalized around the concept of the Goddess – instilled by the paradigm of the One True Father God of patriarchy. Despite our varied spiritual paths, we aligned with the understanding that women need not believe in the Goddess in literal or religious terms in order to benefit from her archetypical wisdom. Instead, we embraced the Goddess as an embodiment of the energy of feminine and female sovereignty, power, dignity and sacredness; we saw the characterizations of the multicultural Divine Feminine throughout history *reflected within ourselves*.

The Goddess meditations that I wrote for the mother-daughter circles are the focus of this section, adapted to reflect the depth of experience of the adult woman. I have included a selection of Goddesses from many cultures, each of whom represents a quality that we may want to nurture and strengthen in ourselves. I invite you now to join me on the path of the Goddess, and take the next step in your wild and wise Sacred Feminine journey.

ARTEMIS –
AUTHENTICITY

he Greek Goddess of the wildwood and the moon, Artemis is the unmistakable archetype of the self-possessed woman: a woman unto herself. With her iconic bow and arrow, Artemis stands ready to unapologetically claim what she wants and needs and is practiced in the art of focusing her energy with precision in the direction of her goals. When we embody the wild wisdom of Artemis, we give ourselves permission to step into our sovereignty, to know ourselves fully, and to live our truth with absolute authenticity.

MEDITATION

Allow yourself to relax completely, and take a deep breath in. As you release it, imagine yourself walking through a beautiful forest. It is late evening, almost dark, but the bright full moon above casts a magical halo over your surroundings. In the trees you see owls, nodding wisely in your direction. On the path ahead of you, you see a regal stag, standing still and proud. He looks at you, and you sense that he wants you to follow him. You walk together to a small clearing. In the light of the moon you see the Goddess Artemis standing with her bow and arrow, her hunting dog at her side. She is waiting for you.

"Welcome sister," she says. "Walk with me and I will share my story. My father Zeus is King of all Gods, and powerful beyond measure. On my third birthday, he asked me what I most wanted, and knowing he had the power to grant me any wish, I told him that I wanted to be forever free, to remain whole and unclaimed by another. I wanted to be my own person. I knew then, as I know now, what I needed for my own fulfillment and for the most authentic manifestation of my personhood."

"Was that difficult for your father to agree to?" you ask, imagining the typical response of a father in our culture to that type of request.

"Not at all," Artemis replies. "Unlike your reality, we Gods and Goddesses are not bound by the constraints of culture; we are not compelled by a concern for approval or a sense of obligation to the status quo. Because conformity is not valued here, I am not limited in my choices by the stereotypes that have been created in your culture – stereotypes that are perpetuated to dampen your power and keep you contained. I am free to unapologetically choose my own path, to determine my own goals, and to focus my energy as powerfully as this arrow in the direction of my truth."

You hear the words of Artemis with admiration and awe, imagining what your life would be like if you gave yourself permission to step beyond the limitations of our culture and express yourself with complete authenticity.

You tell Artemis, "You have inspired me to reclaim my own authenticity. Can you help me?"

Artemis says, "I am a midwife, sister; of course I can support you in birthing your most authentic self. *You were born as I was*: whole and complete unto yourself. It is only because of your experience as a woman in a patriarchal society that you have been persuaded to forget this – but the fact still remains. You have the power of the arrow as well, the power to focus your energy on what matters most to you and to move authentically in the direction of your truth – without apology. Now that you know it is yours to claim, you need not hand over your arrow to anyone, ever again."

You allow Artemis' message to sink deep into your spirit, and commit to remembering the truth of her wisdom as you practice claiming your own authenticity and channeling your truth.

Artemis tells you that it is now time to return. You walk with her back to the clearing, and down the path where you saw the stag and the owls. As you reach the end of your journey, Artemis turns to face you, and says, "I honor your journey, sister, and I am always with you. Remember that you are invited to return here anytime you need to reconnect with your wholeness and authenticity."

She kisses you on the cheek, and walks back into the moonlit forest. You walk back down the path, returning, returning to your body here and now. When you are ready, open your eyes. Welcome back!

FOR DEEPER REFLECTION

What cultural messages have you internalized about your ability to live authentically?

In what ways are you currently preventing yourself from aligning with your truth?

What would it feel like to give yourself permission to focus your energy in the direction of your truth?

APHRODITE –
SACRED SEXUALITY

*A*phrodite, the Greek Goddess of love and sexuality, is *a familiar archetype. Born of the union between sky and sea, she is often depicted emerging nude from the ocean, and has served as muse for countless artists. Like Artemis, Aphrodite is unabashed in the expression of her authentic self; her mythology abounds with lovers – a reflection of Aphrodite's inherent acceptance of her beautifully sensual and magnetic nature. When we embody the wild wisdom of Aphrodite, we give ourselves permission to connect with and cultivate our sacred sexuality, to overwrite the patriarchal narrative around women's pleasure, and tap into one of our most potent and powerful connections to Source.*

MEDITATION

Take a deep breath and allow yourself to sink fully into relaxation. Feel yourself supported and held, and follow your breath as it ebbs and flows. As you listen to your breath, you become aware of the sound of waves upon the shore, and you feel the weight of your body sinking into the sand.

You are at the ocean, sitting comfortably on the beach, taking in all of the details of your surroundings. Further along the shoreline, you see a woman, and she is walk-ing toward you. Immediately you realize that she is nude, and you sense her absolute comfort and ease in her unclothed state. She is beautiful... and her beauty emanates not only from her physical self, but from her undeniable empowered embodiment.

You feel drawn to her, and she smiles as you begin to walk toward her.

"My sister!" she says when you are finally face to face. "I have been waiting for you. Walk with me?" You walk in silence for a short time, and then she says,

"I am Aphrodite, Goddess of love and beauty and sexu-ality. I've come with an important message for you. But first, a question: How's your sex life?"

You laugh at her audacity... but are too intrigued by this conversation to deny a response. You answer with complete honesty.

Aphrodite listens with her whole heart, and when you have shared your truth completely, she speaks.

"In your story, I hear the echoes of every woman; I hear the stories I've heard for the past two millennia. Stories of sadness, shame, denial, taboo, and disconnection. Sto-ries of doubt, of trauma, of apathy and ambiguity. Your culture has robbed you of the precious birthright of your sexual pleasure as a woman, and I am here to help you reclaim your Aphrodite essence."

"But... I don't know how to find that within myself," you say.

Aphrodite responds, "It is there; it has always been there. Your primary sexual relationship is with *yourself*... any other relationship of a sexual nature is merely a reflection of this truth."

As soon as she speaks the words, you feel them deep

within your spirit. You know that she is right. You think back to the messages you have heard and internalized about your own sexual pleasure, from childhood onward. You feel the mixed messages our society feeds us about being both hypersexual objects and chaste virgins. You begin to make sense of the vilification and branding of women who have the courage to step into their sexual power and to claim their pleasure prerogative.

As the message of the Goddess sinks even deeper into your psyche, you feel an awakening within yourself. Much like Aphrodite's birth from the clamshell, you feel the opening and emergence of your own sexual Goddess within.

With complete authority, you begin to make space for this vital aspect of your whole self. You allow yourself to connect fully with this wild and wise part of you, and you give her permission to express her wants and needs. You hear her, and you feel her.

You sense in your physical body the need and desire for pleasure; for *your* pleasure. You know that your sexual needs are beautiful and divine, and above all, they are your birthright.

Aphrodite speaks again, and says, "Now that you know the truth about the power of your pleasure, allow no man or God to come between you and your sacred sexuality. Prioritize your pleasure without apology, sister, and know that in doing so, you will unleash a part of yourself that is more divinely potent than you've ever imagined."

You feel Aphrodite's words swell within you, pulsing in rhythm with the ocean tide at your feet. You take a moment to memorize this feeling, this connection, this activation of your deepest self, and Aphrodite reminds you that you can return here anytime you need to reconnect and remember.

With a bow of gratitude, you offer Aphrodite your deepest thanks for her message. You begin your walk up the beach, knowing you are forever changed by this experience.

As you walk, you begin to shift your awareness to your breath, feeling your body here and now. You begin to gently return to your body, moving with ease. When you are ready, open your eyes. Welcome back!

FOR DEEPER REFLECTION

What cultural messages have you internalized about your sexuality/sexual pleasure?

In what ways are you currently preventing yourself from prioritizing your sexual fulfillment?

What would it feel like to give yourself permission to cultivate and explore a sexual relationship with yourself?

BRIGID –
INSPIRATION

he Celtic Goddess of fire, Brigid is the keeper of the sacred fire of inspiration. Born with a crown of flame atop her head, Brigid invites you to tend to your inner wildfire and fan the flames of your expressive and creative passion. Brigid's stature as a sacred metalsmith reflects her ability to masterfully harness the elements to forge new creations, demonstrating the power of energetic transmutation. When we embody the wild wisdom of Brigid, we say yes to our passion, we cultivate a connection with our unique gifts, we make space and time to tend to our sacred wildfire, and we activate healing through creative expression.

MEDITATION

Take a deep breath and relax your body. As you exhale, imagine yourself walking on a path that leads into a cave. Walking into the mouth of the cave, you notice a flaming torch on the wall, so you take it in hand and begin to walk into the depths of the cavern. Deeper and deeper you go, curious but not afraid, with your torchlight to guide you. As you walk deeper, you notice a source of light, which gets brighter as you walk toward it. As you get closer, you realize it is the light of a bright and beautiful fire, which is burning in the center of a spacious but inviting cavern. Unlike the rest of the cave, this room is decorated beautifully and richly. Take a moment now to notice the details of this womb-like space.

As you are admiring the adornments of the space, you notice a beautiful woman entering the cavern – she is a woman unlike any you have seen. She has long wavy red hair, and beautiful flames atop her head. She says, "Hello beloved sister. I am Brigid, Goddess of Inspiration. I am keeper of the fire that fuels your wild feminine spirit, and inspires the creative expression of your unique gifts."

"My unique gifts?" you ask.

"Yes," she says. "Each of us is born with a special gift that we are meant to share with the world; it is our life's purpose to discover our gift and to let our inner light radiate and shine like the light of my fire. We do this when we connect passionately to our ecstatic 'yes' energy. That is how we know that we are experiencing alignment with our purpose."

She notices that you are intrigued, and continues, "Tell me something that you love to do. Something that makes your spirit soar, and your heart sing. Tell me what makes you feel completely lost in the moment. What makes you feel free, and whole, and connected to your own inherent wild feminine?"

As you tell her all about it, you see that the fire in the center of the cavern is growing bigger, and brighter, and hotter! You also feel a radiant heat in your core, in your womb-space, mirroring the light and heat of the fire in the room.

Brigid smiles, and points to the fire. "Do you see that? *That* is your ecstatic 'yes' energy! That is the fire of inspiration! This is the fuel that you will use for the rest of your life, the fire that will lead you to the most authentic expression of your unique gifts. The fire that will inspire you to create the life you were meant to live. It will always be a part of you, and you can give yourself permission to fuel the flames by staying connected to your 'yes' energy on a regular basis. Staying connected to your wild feminine fire is essential to your well-being as a woman. Make a practice of checking in with the fire in your womb-space, and noticing when it needs the breath of life to fan the flames. Don't be afraid to say 'yes' to whatever nourishes that fire, my beloved sister. The fire is more valuable than a compass, lighting your way along your journey."

Brigid then picks up a glowing ember from the heart of the fire, and holds it in her hands, telling you, "This is an ember from your wild and wise feminine fire, my sister. This ember will never die, and will always be here to inspire and guide you. Shift your attention to this ember if you are ever feeling disconnected from your wild and wise Sacred Feminine spirit, and know that just by saying 'yes' to feeding this ember, you can make your fire beautiful and radiant once again."

You place the ember in your pouch, and thank Brigid for her gift.

You then begin walking back up to the mouth of the cave, moving toward the light with each step. When you reach the entrance, your focus shifts back to your body, here in this moment, and you begin to gently move. When you are ready, open your eyes. Welcome back!

FOR DEEPER REFLECTION

What cultural messages have you internalized about your creative expression?

In what ways are you currently preventing yourself from prioritizing your ecstatic yes?

What would it feel like to give yourself permission to share your gifts with the world?

CERRIDWEN –
DEATH & REBIRTH

erridwen, the Welsh Goddess of death and rebirth, challenges our modern western perspective that life and time are linear – with a specific starting point and a definite end – and instead invites us to embrace the cyclical example of nature. Death ensures new life; endings beget beginnings. When we embody the wild wisdom of Cerridwen, we welcome alignment with the timeless rhythms of nature, and we open to the perspective that each ending ushers in the potency of a new beginning.

MEDITATION

Take a deep breath in, and as you exhale, feel your entire body relax. Connect with your breath, observing each inhale and exhale, and connect with the beautiful pulse of your heartbeat. As you feel that rhythm, and hear that rhythm, you become aware that you can hear the sound of your footsteps on a path. Walking through the fragrant stillness of a forest, you notice a bright clearing up ahead, and continue walking with a sense of anticipation and curiosity.

You emerge from the forest into a vast meadow of golden grasses and wildflowers, one of the most beautiful sights you have ever seen. You take a moment to walk along the edge of this breathtaking meadow, noticing the many varieties of grasses and flowers, and the creatures who call this place home.

As you continue to walk, you notice far up ahead a large patch of blackened earth, smoke still gently rising into the sky. Feeling concerned, you walk quickly toward the far edge of this meadow, and realize that the wildflowers and grasses have been lost to a fire.

Sadness fills your heart as you contemplate this once thriving habitat… and you see movement out of the corner of your eye. At the boundary where the charred ground meets the still-vibrant meadow, you see an old crone with a small torch, leaning into the grasses and setting them aflame.

"Stop!" you yell. "Don't destroy the meadow!"

The crone stops and turns toward you, and you see that she is Cerridwen, the Goddess of Death and Rebirth. You notice everything about her appearance: her clothing, her hair, her eyes.

"Ah, sister," she says. "I have been expecting you. But I am not *destroying* the meadow, beloved… I am merely transforming it. You see, in the vast expanse of the universe, there is really no such thing as destruction… there is change, there is transmutation."

"But," you say, "if you burn the meadow, it will die! The flowers will die… the grasses will die… It's not right!"

"Yes, that is true that there will be death," says Cerridwen, "but this death will indeed be the catalyst for new life. The soil cannot be fertile for next year's growth without the ash and the composted leaves and plants of this year's meadow. The seeds of the beautiful golden grasses will not crack open to allow new sprouts unless they are burned by the heat of a fire. This death is merely the next phase in the cycle of the *life* of this meadow. Just as we watch the moon wax and wane each month, and see the coming and going of the seasons each year, and experience the building and release of our wombs with each cycle, we women know that death and rebirth go hand-in-hand. Nothing can endure forever, and endings are beautiful in their own way. Yes, we grieve, and we feel sadness when we experience an ending, but we must also reflect on the beauty of each moment of aliveness that we were able to witness, or experience. We treasure the gifts of that life, and with gratitude we are able to accept when the cycle is complete, and when the time for death has come. We then watch as What Once Was transforms into What Will Be. Transformation is the miracle of this planet, beloved, and you hold within you the power of transformation as well. Your path to wisdom means learning when to let go, to accept endings, and to transform that energy into the rebirth of something new."

As you internalize Cerridwen's words, you turn back and look at the part of the meadow that is now covered in ash and seeds, seeing the scene with new eyes. Rather than seeing merely death, you see the amazing potential of the meadow-to-come. You see Mama Earth, preparing for her winter rest, doing her work of composting and germinating. You see the seeds, shells cracked and ready to take root and sprout. You see the energy of the flowers and grasses, released back into the soil, becoming the nourishment for future life. But more than all of this… you see beauty. You see wisdom. You see the miracle of transformation.

With a last glance of deep appreciation, you offer a

bow of thanks to Cerridwen for her wisdom. She acknowledges and returns your bow, and returns to her work as you make your way back up the path. Gently now, your awareness returns to this space and time, and you feel ready to open your eyes. Welcome back!

FOR DEEPER REFLECTION

What cultural messages have you internalized about death and endings?

In what ways are you currently preventing yourself from releasing what no longer serves you?

What would it feel like to give yourself permission to cultivate an appreciation for the potency of endings?

HATHOR –
PLEASURE

athor, the Egyptian Goddess of bodily pleasure, was one of the most revered deities of her region, and was honored for over 3000 years. Depicted with a woman's body and the head or horns of a cow, Hathor was credited with creating the physical body to house our immortal soul, and graced humans with all physical pleasures such as sound, music, song, dance, art, love, taste, smell and touch. So beloved was she that more festivals were held in her honor than any other deity of her time. Celebrations related to Hathor focused on dancing, singing, food and drink, and entertainment... all things joyful and pleasurable. When we embody the wild wisdom of Hathor, we give ourselves permission to prioritize our pleasure, to attend to the sensual experience of our embodiment, and to practice the art of sacred self-care.

MEDITATION

Take a deep breath, and as you exhale, imagine yourself floating on a beautiful boat along the River Nile in Egypt. Gently rocking from side to side, your canopied boat travels gently along the river, traveling slowly past many beautiful stone temples. Your boat comes to a gentle stop at the foot of a walkway that leads up to a beautiful temple, and you step, with bare feet, out onto the warm marble walkway. As you walk toward the temple, you notice all of the details of the intricate exterior… the type of stone, the carvings or words etched into the façade, the shape and size of the building itself. Feeling welcomed and expected, you step into the sanctuary of this temple, and are immediately filled with pleasure. As you look all around, you notice the lavishly adorned space… the sounds that you hear… the delicious food and drink set on a table for you… and then you notice the Goddess Hathor, reclining luxuriously in the place of honor.

Hathor smiles at you and says, "Welcome, beloved sister. I have been waiting for you. You have been invited into my temple so that I may teach you the importance of pleasure." You thank Hathor and ask her to share what you have come to learn.

"Pleasure," she says, "is a fundamental aspect of our well-being, but something that is undervalued in your culture. Without pleasure, our lives become monotonous and gray… we lose our passion and creativity and our deep inner joy. As women, we are taught that focusing on our own pleasure is selfish… but this could not be further from the truth. Nourishing our well-being by making time for pleasure is one of the most important things we can do for ourselves. And despite what we may have been told, it is healthy for others as well; for as we experience pleasure, we radiate our well-being, and give others permission to prioritize their pleasure as well. When we take time to fill ourselves up with pleasure, we can give to others from a place of abundance rather than obligation."

"But how do we prioritize our pleasure when so many of us have completely lost touch with the concept of pleasure?" you ask.

"I'm glad you asked," Hathor replies. "For today we are going to have a day filled with pure pleasure, just for you. Your day can be filled with *anything* you would like to do, and because time does not exist in this space, the day can last as long as you'd like. Tell me now, sister, how will you experience pleasure today?"

You spend time telling Hathor, in detail, how you would like to spend the day, knowing that your pleasure is the only thing on the agenda.

Hathor replies, "That sounds delicious. And so it is."

After spending the timeless day nourishing yourself with everything that brings you pleasure, you are filled with a deep sense of fulfillment and joy. You thank Hathor for teaching you the wisdom of pleasure, and embrace her before you step back onto the walkway that will take you to your boat. Hathor reminds you that you may return whenever you need to remember the importance of your pleasure, and invites you to commit to a practice of prioritizing your pleasure.

You step into your boat once again, and begin your journey back up the river. Gently floating up and up, until you are fully embodied once again, here in this moment. Welcome back!

FOR DEEPER REFLECTION

What cultural messages have you internalized about your right to experience pleasure?

In what ways are you currently preventing yourself from prioritizing your pleasure?

What would it feel like to give yourself permission to cultivate a practice of pleasure?

DURGA –
BOUNDARIES

The Hindu Goddess of protection, Durga is a fierce warrior with eight arms – each brandishing one of her divine weapons. Riding her lion into battle, Durga is charged with safeguarding all that is sacred and protecting the peace. The name Durga in Sanskrit translates as "fortress," evoking a sense of strength and safety. When we embody the wild wisdom of Durga, we give ourselves permission to create and uphold healthy boundaries, to honor our limitations, and to choose who and what we allow into our inner sanctum.

MEDITATION

Close your eyes, and take a deep breath in. Exhale and imagine yourself walking up a hill. You feel yourself climbing up, until you reach the top of the footpath. Before you, you see that the top of the hill is flat and wide. As you observe your surroundings, the Goddess Durga comes to greet you. "Welcome to my sanctuary," she says. She offers her hand, and you walk together toward the middle of the hilltop. As you walk, Durga speaks. "This hilltop is my sacred domain. Visitors are allowed only by invitation. You can be sure that you are safe and at peace here. I have invited you here to learn the ways of boundary-making."

"Unlike cultures past, women in your world are not taught and encouraged to develop healthy boundaries; to know with certainty where you end, and another begins. You were never invited to cultivate a line that you let no other cross. Despite what you have learned as a woman in this culture, your innate impulse to create and uphold healthy boundaries is your inherent right. You knew as a child without being told that healthy boundaries are the key to keeping yourself whole and safe. Your wild wisdom knew then, and still knows, when it is safe to let people in, and it warns you when you must keep someone out. Since childhood, though, you have been taught to disconnect from this aspect of yourself; to silence and ignore your truth. But not any longer: today, you will create your boundaries and begin the practice of protecting your sacred inner space. Without apology."

You respond to Durga, "Yes, I am ready. I have always been ready. How do we begin?"

Durga says, "First, look all around us. Feel the space, decide how large you would like your boundary to be. It can be hundreds of feet around us, or it can be just at your fingertips.

"Now that you have decided on your space, it is time to create a border. Your border can be anything you choose... it can be a clear bubble, strong as glass; or it can be a wall of fire. It can be a hedge of roses, with dangerous thorns... or it can be a shroud of mist. Whatever it is, create it now."

You look all around, and as you look, your boundary is created. Your sacred space is safely enclosed. As you look at the border that you have created, you notice a door, which is shut and locked. And Durga reminds you, "No one can enter your sacred space without your permission. Your practice now is to allow yourself to create and uphold healthy boundaries – even when you are compelled by others to do otherwise. *Especially* when you are compelled by others to do otherwise."

You commit to protecting your sacred inner space by creating and maintaining healthy boundaries, and thank Durga for sharing her wisdom.

Durga reminds you that you can return to this safe and sacred space anytime you need to, and then walks with you back toward the path. Together, you walk down the hill, retracing your steps to the bottom.

When you reach the end of the path, Durga hugs you, and you feel her power and strength melt into your body. She waves goodbye to you as she begins her journey back up the path. With a smile, you wave goodbye, and gently begin to return to your body, here in this moment. When you are ready, open your eyes. Welcome back!

FOR DEEPER REFLECTION

What cultural messages have you internalized about creating and upholding healthy boundaries?

In what ways are you currently preventing yourself from developing or honoring your own boundaries?

What would it feel like to give yourself permission to prioritize your boundaries?

SEKHMET –
RAGE

he lion-headed Goddess of Rage, Sekhmet is perhaps one of the oldest and most widely recognized deities in the Egyptian pantheon. Sekhmet was summoned by her father, Ra the Sun God, to punish mankind for not following his law. Sekhmet channeled her righteous rage in response to the imbalance and injustice that was inflicted by humans upon the world. When we embody the wild wisdom of Sekhmet, we grant ourselves permission to feel and express the full spectrum of human emotions and release the transformative power of our rage.

MEDITATION

Sit or lie comfortably, and take a deep breath in. As you exhale, feel yourself sinking heavily, fully supported by sand. As you begin to become aware of your surroundings, you realize that you are in the desert, with nothing but dunes in every direction and the sun high in the sky. On your skin, you feel the heat of the sun; in your heart, you feel despair for the state of the world.

As you scan the horizon, you see a figure walking toward you – with the body of a woman, and the head of a lioness. Upon her head rests a crown adorned with the golden disk of the sun, and you recognize her as the Goddess Sekhmet.

"Greetings, sister," she says. "Why have you come here, to sit alone in the vast emptiness of the desert?"

"I am here because I can no longer live in this world. I can't bear the injustice and imbalance any longer. There is nothing I can do about any of it. So I came here."

"Aaahh," Sekhmet says. "I understand. You have never been taught the transformative power of your rage. You, like all women of your culture, have been taught only to repress your anger, to deny your powerful feelings and dwell instead in the patriarchy-approved feelings of sadness and despair."

After pondering this for a moment, you reply, "Yes… I think you are right. From my earliest memories, I was told time and again that my anger was not allowed. My right to feel rage was taken from me, and was given over completely to the domain of boys and men… just as their sadness was taken from them and given over to me. And now all I know how to feel is sad!"

Sekhmet says, "Despite everything you've been conditioned to believe, your feelings of anger and rage are valuable. Anger is a potent warning that deserves your attention and response. Rage in the face of injustice is one of the most powerful forces in the world – and it is needed now more than ever."

"But it's too late," you say. "I was robbed of my rage, and now it's gone."

"No," says Sekhmet, "It isn't gone. Just as the sun is hidden from view each night only because of your limited human perspective, your rage is a force of nature that can never be taken from you."

You reflect on Sekhmet's words, and feel the intense heat of the desert sun. As the external heat intensifies, you begin to feel the internal heat of the unexpressed rage that has always been within you. You remember this feeling, and you resist the urge to keep the rage in, to tamp it down or transmute it to despair as you have been taught to do.

"Let it out, sister," Sekhmet says. "Holding you rage within harms you, and it does not serve the well-being of the world. Only by shifting your rage outward – *to outrage* – can you harness your innate power of transformation."

With these words, you feel the heat of your anger and rage shift outward, out of your body, merging with the energetic vibrations of justice and balance. You support the release of this energy by moving your body or opening your voice in the way that feels most powerful.

When you have discharged the full extent of your rage, you lie quietly in the sand, feeling spent but at peace.

Sekhmet says, "This is the way of healing, sister: feeling and releasing our anger. Owning and channeling our rage to activate change. This process is your birthright, and an integral part of the global rebalancing that is needed now. Let no one tell you otherwise."

You inhale deeply, inviting this wisdom to integrate fully into your spirit. You thank Sekhmet for the gift of rage, and she bows in recognition of the Divine within you and reminds you that you can return to her anytime you need to reconnect with your anger and rage. As she walks away, you commit to a practice of respecting *all* of your feelings, knowing they are a crucial and powerful aspect of your Sacred Feminine spirit.

With another deep inhale and exhale, you begin to shift your awareness back to your body, back to this moment. Gently returning to this space and time, you open your eyes. Welcome back!

FOR DEEPER REFLECTION

What cultural messages have you internalized about your expression of anger and rage?

In what ways are you currently preventing yourself from releasing these feelings?

What would it feel like to give yourself permission to reclaim the transformational power of your outrage?

GWENHWYFAR –
SOVEREIGNTY

oddess of Wales, Gwenhwyfar is most recognized
as Queen Guinevere, the beloved consort of King
Arthur. The very symbol of the Welsh land and
throne itself, Guinevere's sovereignty was coveted by many
who wished to claim the kingdom for themselves. When we
embody the wild wisdom of Gwenhwyfar, we step into the
sovereignty that is our birthright, and fully inhabit the seat
of our Sacred Feminine power.

MEDITATION

Close your eyes and take a deep breath in. As you breathe
out, imagine you are walking through a beautiful garden
alongside a magnificent castle. All around, trees and
flowers are in bloom. You continue walking, and come
into a clearing in the garden, where you see a queen, and
you recognize her as Gwenhwyfar. You notice what she
looks like: her eyes, her hair, what she is wearing. In her
hand, you see that she is holding a sword.

"Welcome to my domain, beloved sister," she says. "I
am Queen Gwenhwyfar, and I have been waiting for
you."

"Where are we?" you ask the Queen.

"In Camelot," she replies, "where I reign as Sovereign. I am the personification of this very land, and no man rules here without my consent."

You nod, and then ask about her sword. "This sword keeps me free of the bindings that others try to place upon me. Because I am sovereign and allow none to rule above me, there are those who wish to diminish my power by energetically binding me. Some may try to control my emotions by placing a bind around my heart; I can use my sword to cut it. Some may try to control my thoughts by placing a bind around my mind; I can use my sword to cut it. Some may try to control my words by placing a bind around my throat or over my mouth; I can use my sword to cut it. Because I am aware of my innate sovereignty, there is no bind more powerful than I am."

You ask Gwenhwyfar what other types of bindings you might use the sword to cut, and she tells you.

You tell her that you had never realized that throughout your life, countless energetic binds have been placed upon you by others wishing to control and contain your power.

"Of course you didn't know!" she says. "Only by keeping you unaware of your sovereignty can others control you. The messages you see and hear every day about what it means to be a woman are designed to keep you ignorant of your power: bound and compliant. Their worst fear is that you will learn the truth: that you are innately sovereign."

"And now... I know," you say.

"Yes," says Gwenhwyfar, "and now that you know, you have a most sacred assignment: to show your sisters, and your daughters, how to claim their sovereignty and cut their binds."

You commit to a practice of stepping into your inherent power by claiming your sovereignty, knowing that in doing so, you will teach other women to do the same.

"It is time for your return," the Queen says.

She then begins to lead you back down the path on which you came, quietly walking until you are nearly at the beginning again. She turns and hands you the sword that she holds; you examine the sword and notice what it is made of. You examine the handle, and notice its shape and size. The Queen says, "This sword represents your sovereignty. Use it to cut any bindings that others try to place upon you. Do not let your emotions, or your thoughts, or your feelings be controlled by others. You are wild, and wise, and unbound."

You thank Gwenhwyfar, and she smiles at you. As she walks back down the path, you take a deep breath and open your eyes. Welcome back!

FOR DEEPER REFLECTION

What cultural messages have you internalized about the idea of personal sovereignty?

In what ways are you currently preventing yourself from claiming your sovereignty?

What would it feel like to give yourself permission to reclaim your inherent sovereignty?

MAYA –
ILLUSION

aya, considered the Mother of Creation by her devotees in India, is the Hindu and Buddhist Goddess of illusion. Having magically brought all of nature into existence simply by willing it so, Maya knows the truth of existence beyond the veils of our human perception of separateness, and teaches us that we are all one. When we embody the wild wisdom of Maya and see past the illusion of the material world, we connect with the magic of our deepest spiritual selves, and we see ourselves as the radiant manifestation of the Divine.

MEDITATION

Lie comfortably, and inhale deeply. As you breathe out, imagine that you are lying on a cloud floating above the earth. You breathe in and float so comfortably on your cloud, and notice that you are covered in several silky veils, from head to toe. The veils feel soft against your skin, and because they are all different colors, they give everything you see a luminous glow from your view in the clouds.

Looking beside you, you see the Goddess Maya sitting on her own cloud. She smiles and welcomes you to her domain. She tells you that she has invited you here to learn about your true self, and has covered you in veils to help you understand the power of illusion.

You tell her that you already know your true self, and Maya says, "But do you? You may know who you are according to your society. You may have adopted a persona based on what the patriarchy directs your attention toward: external appearance, conformity, and consumption. These are nothing more than tools, practical ways of controlling women and keeping them disconnected from the vastness of their Sacred Feminine spirit."

You look unsure, so Maya says, "Let's do an experiment then."

And she asks, "If I wanted to know the true you, should I look at your house?"

You respond, "No, where I live is not who I am."

Maya removes the first veil from your body, and lets it float down and down, disappearing below you.

She asks, "If I wanted to know the true you, would I look at the clothes you wear?"

You respond, "No, what I wear is not who I am."

Maya removes the second veil from your body, and lets it float down and down, disappearing below you.

She asks, "If I wanted to know the true you, would I look at the things that you own?

You respond, "No, my things are not who I am."

Maya removes the third veil from your body, and lets it float down and down, disappearing below you.

She asks, "If I wanted to know the true you, would I look at your hair?"

You respond, "No, my hair is not who I am."

Maya removes the fourth veil from your body, and lets it float down and down, disappearing below you.

She asks, "If I wanted to know the true you, would I look at your body – your skin, your cells, your blood, your bones?

You respond, "No, my body is not who I am."

Maya removes the fifth veil from your body, and lets it float down and down, disappearing below you.

She asks, "If I wanted to know the true you, would I listen to your thoughts?"

You respond, "No, my thoughts are not who I am."

Maya removes the last veil from your body, and lets it float down and down, disappearing below you.

And now, after all the veils have been removed, Maya sees a beautiful glow emanating from you. You are shining from the inside, a bright beautiful light. The light becomes so radiant, that Maya sees only the light of your soul.

Maya asks, "If I wanted to know the true you, would I see your inner light?

You respond, "Yes… my inner light is the reflection of my Sacred Feminine spirit. *This* is the essence of who I am."

"Yes," says Maya, "and as it is for you, so it is for everyone. We are all One, each of us the beautifully prismatic expression of the Divine. Do not let the veils of illusion – such as how you dress, where you live, the color of your skin, or what you own – prevent you from knowing yourself, and knowing others, as intrinsically Divine."

You allow the truth of Maya's words to sink deep into your spirit, expanding your awareness exponentially, and commit to bringing this new-found awareness into your daily practice.

Maya lets you know that it is time to return, and you thank her for sharing her wild wisdom with you. You begin floating down, back down into your body in this place and time. When you are ready, open your eyes. Welcome back!

FOR DEEPER REFLECTION

What cultural messages have you internalized about the locus of your identity?

In what ways are you currently preventing yourself from experiencing your true spiritual nature?

What would it feel like to give yourself permission to cultivate a practice of expanding your spiritual awareness?

LAKSHMI –
ABUNDANCE

he beloved Indian Goddess of prosperity and good fortune, Lakshmi is often depicted in a lotus flower upon an ocean of milk, holding symbols of abundance in three of her four hands, while her fourth hand is open in a gesture of receiving. Offering her blessings of material and spiritual wealth, Lakshmi is the mother of manifestation. When we embody the wild wisdom of Lakshmi, we actively magnetize what it is we wish to call in, we release our deeply-ingrained scarcity mentality, and we trust that all of our needs will be met with divine timing.

MEDITATION

Take a deep breath in and allow yourself to fully release all tension in your body as you exhale. Follow the natural ebb and flow of your breath for a few cycles... and begin to notice the sound of waves upon the shore, matching the rhythm of your breath.

From your vantage upon high sand dunes, you look upon an ocean – not of saltwater, however. This ocean is made of milk... the timeless symbol of abundance.

As you gaze into the vast sea, you notice that there is a larger-than-life lotus blossoming on the surface, and at the center of the bloom, sits a beautiful woman. Unlike a human woman, however, she has four arms – and you recognize her immediately as Lakshmi, the Goddess of Abundance. Holding a flower in one hand and a bowl overflowing with milk in another, Lakshmi asks why you have come to her shores.

You respond, "I have come to seek your guidance, Goddess, because I am experiencing a lack, a scarcity."

Lakshmi says, "Tell me, what is it that you do not have enough of?" and you answer her.

Lakshmi nods knowingly, and says, "I want to tell you a secret – one that many masters know, but that humans rarely believe. The universe is wise in that it always responds to our words, and conspires to validate the things we say and think. If your practice is to dwell on thoughts and words that reflect scarcity and lack, the universe will certainly make that so. If you habitually say, 'I don't have enough money,' then you will not have enough money. If you habitually think, 'I don't have real and lasting love,' then you will not have real and lasting love. If your mindset is perpetually focused on your physical ailments, you will experience perpetual physical ailments. If you feel as though you never have enough time, you will experience life as though you are in a constant race against the clock."

"But the universe is itself a place of eternal abundance! It is all-providing, and there is always enough. Enough money, enough love, enough health, enough time."

You look at Lakshmi, dubious, and say, "I really don't think it's that easy."

Lakshmi says, "I know you don't, dear sister, but that is only because you were never taught otherwise. What would you do if you knew that changing your life is as simple as shifting your perspective? What if you knew that in order to receive, the first and most important step is to simply thank the universe for whatever it is you feel you lack, knowing that in doing so, you affirm that it will be provided?"

Skeptical, you ask Lakshmi to give you an example.

"Hold out your left hand," she says, "and think for a moment about what you lack. Take a breath, and offer heart-felt gratitude to the universe for providing what you need with such ease and grace."

You look to your upturned left palm, and find that something is now there. You feel a sense of awe and wonder.

Lakshmi says, "Remember, sister, abundance is the way of the loving universe. We can easily tap into this abundance by simply making a practice of offering thanks for gifts that are already on their way, and opening with intention and gratitude to receive them."

She then takes a drop of milk from her bowl, which magically transforms into a mother-of-pearl bead, and places it into your pouch. You thank Lakshmi for her wisdom, and listen once again to the sound of the waves upon the shore.

Connecting now to your own breath in this time and space, you become aware of your body. Moving with ease, you return to your body in your own time. Welcome back!

FOR DEEPER REFLECTION

What cultural messages have you internalized about abundance and scarcity?

In what ways are you currently preventing yourself from experiencing the abundance of the universe?

What would it feel like to give yourself permission to expect abundance?

LUNA –
CYCLES

onored in Roman culture for countless generations, *Luna, the moon Goddess, is revered for her rhythmic illumination. Associated with female blood myster-ies and cycles, the moon is the source of our monthly hormonal ebb and flow, and her full luminance often aligns with birth. When we embody the wild wisdom of Luna, we honor our cyclical female nature, we connect with the natural rhythm of our bodies, and we invite sacred illumination.*

MEDITATION

Close your eyes and take a deep breath in, allowing your body to fully relax. Take a moment to follow your breath… and to connect with the beating of your heart. As you hear that steady rhythm, imagine you are hearing the sound of your own footsteps on a path as you walk on a beautiful moonlit night. This path can be anywhere that feels most safe and sacred to you; it can be on the sandy shores of a beach, in an ancient forest, atop a majestic mountain, or anywhere your spirit is called to roam.

As you walk your path, you see the magnificent full moon just above the horizon, hanging like a lantern from the sky; she looks and feels so close that you think you may be able to touch her if you just reach up.

You pause in your walking to stand and gaze with your full attention upon Luna's radiant face, feeling a deep connection and loving bond with this celestial satellite, and feeling within your body a wild and wise stirring.

A sweet breeze shifts past you, and you swear you hear a voice in the wind...

"Sister..." the voice says.

You turn to look for the source of the voice, but see no others near you, and sense that you are indeed the only human present.

You look up again and realize with a deep, resonant knowing, that it is the Moon's voice you hear. You wonder how it is possible that you are hearing the Moon, and she answers your wordless question.

"Yes, you are able to hear me – because we are sisters, as all women are my sisters. Once a part of Mother Earth herself, my body was birthed and set free, into my own orbit, millions of years ago. Never far from our Mother, but on my own journey and my own time, I have watched my Earthly sisters for countless generations.

And because you are made of the same salt-water as the sea, which inherited the gift of my rhythm in her tidal cycle, you too dance with me in a beautiful ebb and flow. Our bodies are connected on this deep physical level, and this indelible rhythm is my gift to my Earthly sisters."

You ponder this, amazed, and then ask, "I see your tidal cycle, but how does my body ebb and flow?"

"Your womb carries this rhythm, from the time you are born until you die. Whether you're a maiden, mother, or crone, the cycle of Luna lives within you, within your spirit and within your cells. The cycles of building, manifesting, and releasing are all within you – energetically, spiritually, and physically. Despite living in your linear culture, where you are taught to repress, deny, and disconnect from your cycle, your connection with me is unbreakable. And by following my rhythm, you can invite new dimensions of well-being into your life.

"My cycle begins anew when my face is dark, the time you know as the new moon. During this phase of renewal, I invite you to harness my energy to plant your seeds of intention, to call down what you want and need, to manifest your deepest desires. In your physical body, this is traditionally the time when women bleed – which many women call their *moon time*. This building time is yours between my dark phase, and the peak of my radiance at the full moon – the time when women traditionally ovulate. The moment after my face is most luminous, I shift into my waning phase; no longer building, but now releasing. Harness the energy of my waning phase to shed what is no longer serving you, as this is a most potent time to unburden yourself of anything you no longer need. By doing so, you create the space for new intentions to be seeded as I shift into renewal once again."

You feel such wonder and awe, knowing that your wild and wise female body embodies this moon magic at every stage of your life. You thank Luna for her beautiful medicine, and she says, "Remember me, sister. I am here in the sky – even when you can't see me – forever connected with our shared rhythm. Look up to my face anytime you need a reminder of your ebb and flow."

You thank Luna for illuminating this beautiful internal wisdom, and commit to integrating the wisdom of the moon into your practice of self-care. With a final deep inhale and exhale, you begin your walk back up the path with a newfound love and appreciation for your female body, and for your connection to the moon. Shifting your awareness now to this space and time, you begin to feel present in your body once more. Moving gently, you open your eyes. Welcome back!

FOR DEEPER REFLECTION

What cultural messages have you internalized about your female cycle?

In what ways are you currently preventing yourself from appreciating your rhythmic nature?

What would it feel like to give yourself permission to cultivate a practice of cyclical awareness and appreciation?

DEMETER – GRIEF & LOSS

Demeter is the ancient Greek Goddess of the harvest, whose abundant bounty fed the people of her region. Demeter's tale is inexorably woven with that of her maiden daughter, Persephone, who was abducted to the Underworld by Hades. Despairing the loss of her daughter, Demeter withdrew from her obligation as guardian of the grains, choosing instead to honor her feelings of grief and loss. When we embody the wild wisdom of Demeter, we give ourselves permission to fully feel and honor our experiences of despair and grief, we resist the cultural narrative about how and when to move forward, and we allow the natural timeline of healing to unfold.

MEDITATION

Take a deep breath and as you exhale, allow yourself to fully sink in, surrendering to the pull of gravity. In this quiet space, you notice the rhythm of your heart beat… and are aware that this rhythm matches the pace of your feet walking along a path. As you scan your environment, you notice immediately the lack of vegetation: nothing is growing where there was once life. As far as the eye can see in every direction, the Earth is dormant.

As you continue to walk, you notice the figure of a woman sitting on the ground up ahead. As you approach, you hear the soft sounds of crying. The woman hears your steps as you draw near, and she wipes her eyes unapologetically as she meets your gaze. "Are you okay?" you ask uncertainly.

"No, sister, I am not. I am grieving; my heart is broken."

Taken aback by her unguarded reply, you are at a loss for words. You had expected the typical response given when pain is inadvertently witnessed: the replacement of tears with a brave face, or an apology for the display of emotion. You had expected anything but the truth.

With a sense of intimacy that only such openness can invite, you ask her to tell her story.

"I am Demeter, Goddess of the Harvest," she begins, "and my daughter Persephone is lost to the Underworld. The loss of my daughter is not something I was prepared for, and my heart has been broken. This grief is all-consuming, and I can no longer focus on my work. Until I can once again preside over the grains, the Earth will remain fallow."

Understanding dawns as you connect the barren landscape with Demeter's grief. But you are curious about something, and you ask her, "How long will you dwell in these feelings, though? Aren't people counting on you to ensure there is food?"

"I will grieve until I am done grieving. Contrary to what you've been taught, there is no timeline for grief. I do not hold myself to the expectation that I will progress through the stages of denial, bargaining, anger, depression, and acceptance in a tidy and predictable fashion; it may take years for me to process my loss. I might experience every stage of grief in one day. It is only in your linear framework that grief is seen as a checklist to complete so that one can 'move on' as soon as possible. Healing doesn't happen that way."

You ponder Demeter's words, and reflect on a time that you have experienced grief and loss. You remember the messages of our society or the people in your community, the implied urgency to swallow your feelings and get on with the rest of your life.

Demeter says, "I'll never understand the taboo in your world against feelings of grief and sadness. These feelings are as natural as all others, but in your world, there is no room made for them. Loss is met with admonitions to 'look on the bright side' or 'find the silver lining,' never with an invitation to take all the time you need to dwell in the fullness of your feelings. Without the benefit of the ability to feel and process your grief and loss, they remain trapped within you – unable to heal, and wounding you repeatedly over time."

Demeter's words ring with a deep knowing inside of you, and you reflect on the pools of unresolved and unexpressed grief that still reside in your being. You wonder how your healing journey may have been different, or may be different still, with permission to fully feel and express your grief – in your own way, in your own time; with permission to step away from your responsibilities and obligations to others, and focus on what *you* most need. For as long as you need.

Demeter rises and takes your hand, and begins walking back up the path from the direction you came.

"This land – my domain – is dormant now, but it won't be forever. I do not fear that I will never return to my life's work; in fact, I know with certainty that I will. But not yet. Not until my season of grief is complete."

With Demeter's words, you see the environment around you with the vision of what will surely be: the grains growing, the flowers blooming, the trees bearing fruit. In the fullness of time, a new season will emerge. But only when this season of grief is honored, allowed, and respected.

As you return to the starting point of your journey, you thank Demeter for sharing her wisdom. She embraces you and reminds you that you can return anytime you need a safe place to feel your grief. As Demeter walks away, you begin to gently return to your body in the here and now. Reinhabiting yourself with ease, you begin moving slowly until you feel fully present and awake. Welcome back!

FOR DEEPER REFLECTION

What cultural messages have you internalized about feeling grief and loss?

In what ways are you currently preventing yourself from experiencing your feelings of grief?

What would it feel like to give yourself permission to fully feel and release your grief?

PART III
THE WHEEL OF THE YEAR

ORIGINS

The Wheel of the Year, prior to the Industrial Age, was the clock and calendar by which all humans abided. Before the artificial light and regimented time zones of the late nineteenth century, we invariably followed the rhythm of the year in terms of when we worked, when we rested, when (and what) we ate, and when we celebrated.

Living in harmony with the rhythm of the seasons, we women were naturally aligned with the external environment – as well as our intrinsic physical and spiritual cycles. But with the introduction of electricity and the deviance from the natural shifts of dark and light, cold and warmth, we were gradually but indisputably disconnected from the spiral dance that had given our lives such depth and meaning.

For many modern women, this loss manifests as an indescribable ache or hunger; a sense that something is missing, but we can't quite put our finger on what it is we lack. Because the legacy of our natural rhythm was lost even before the time of our grandmother's mothers, we don't have a name for what we crave. But we do know that we yearn for *something*.

In the past century and a half, we have been assimilated by the edict of linear time, by page after page of grids and numbers, marching toward infinity with no end in sight. Constant production and consumption have become our national priorities to the detriment of all else. Our bodies feel this; our psyches feel it. Our well-being is depleted as we press on and on, with no natural pause for rest and reflection. Our to-do list is never complete, and despite our never-ending expenditures of energy, it never seems to be enough. We never feel that we are enough.

And like a light bulb left on indefinitely, we too burn out.

But a dawning awareness is spreading among women: an awareness that this linear lifestyle is unsustainable. Inspired by the wild wisdom of the natural world, women are beginning to realign with and reclaim our inherently cyclical nature. The meditations in this section are the intimate expressions of my need to name and claim my hunger, to ground my body and my life in the Wheel of the Year. I invite you to return with me to the richness of our heritage, and relearn the language of our Sacred Feminine legacy.

The Wheel of the Year meditations are based on the seasonal alignment of the Northern Hemisphere. If you are located in the Southern Hemisphere or Equatorial region, I invite you to adapt the flow accordingly.

FOUR SEASONS

aia, the personification of our planet Earth, is the literal mother of all Goddesses, and all of us. Unlike the linear paradigm of patriarchy, Gaia's rhythm is cyclical – as is ours. Each woman holds within her womb-space the quiet potential of winter, the rebirth of spring, the harvest of summer, and the release of autumn. When we embody the wild wisdom of Gaia, we connect with our innate seasonal cycle and invite reverence for our rhythmic Sacred Feminine nature.

MEDITATION

Take a deep breath and allow yourself to fully relax. Follow your breath and prepare to journey back in time... back to the beginning.

In the beginning, God made man in his image. We all know this, we've heard this countless times in our lives. But what of us women? The truth is, we have only heard half of the story. What we haven't been told is that we too were created "in the image of..." but in the image of what? Lush and life-giving, curvaceous and flowing, we are the indisputable daughters of Mother Gaia, the Earth herself. And up until recent generations, there was never any doubt of this; women knew that we were all the sacred daughters of the Great Mother; and men knew this as well.

And in the deep parts of our souls and our bones, we women know this to be true. We feel our connection to the tidal rhythms, to the ebb and flow that connects us to our sister moon.

We see our lives mirrored in the seasons: the youthful promise and potential of maidenhood in spring; the power and creativity of motherhood in summer, the shedding of what no longer serves us during our maven years in autumn, and the wisdom of the crone, going inward during winter.

Our grandmothers' grandmothers knew that our cycles were so much more than the binary "bleeding" or "not bleeding" (as we twenty-first century women have been led to believe). They saw not only the stages of their lives mirrored in the four seasons, but their monthly cycles as well. Gifted with the wild wisdom handed down by their mothers, and their mothers' mothers, our foremothers knew that whether they were menstruating or not, the Great Mother had bestowed upon them an intrinsic hormonal and energetic blueprint, which was the very foundation of their empowered embodiment.

Empowered with the wisdom of autumn, our grandmothers' grandmothers held gratitude for the gift of their bleeding time. They knew without question that it was their birthright to focus on their own needs during this week, to refill the cup from which they had been giving to their families and communities during the previous weeks. They mirrored the falling of the leaves by energetically releasing that which no longer served them. They practiced sacred self-care by slowing down, resting more, and indulging their desires. They knew that the veil to the Otherworld was thinnest during this time, so they enjoyed their increased intuition by journaling, and by going deep into their dream world. Their community honored this time by offering nurturing and extra space to their sisters.

Empowered by the wisdom of winter, our foremothers held gratitude for the gift of the second week of their cycle. They knew that as with the Mother Gaia, the energy was building, quietly but certainly, and that their feminine power was on the verge of peaking. The wise women of our lineage used this week to plant seeds of intention, to build relationships, to focus on projects. Using this kinetic energy, the women connected with their internal and external beauty, ate delicious foods, enjoyed the movement of their bodies, and invested in the community around them. Their community honored this time by choosing their second week to suggest new ideas, to make time to connect, and to reconnect in their relationships.

Empowered by the wisdom of spring, our foremothers held gratitude for their ovulation time. They knew that as with the Great Mother, this was their time to shine! They used this week to put themselves out into the world for all to benefit. This was the week when their ideas and projects had come to fruition, and they held the positive regard of all their community. Our ancestors honored this energy by being open to new things, enjoying flavorful, juicy foods, by expressing themselves energetically and creatively. Their community honored this time by connecting in gratitude for all the gifts that the cycling woman had offered.

Empowered by the wisdom of summer, our foremothers held gratitude for their fourth week, known as the Firewalk. They knew that as with Gaia, the heat and intensity of summer could be dangerous if not respected.

Our ancestors honored this week by recognizing and thanking the emotions that surfaced during this week, and by acknowledging their fiery and passionate predisposition. They chose to limit their energetic output, to stick with familiar routines, and to seek comfort in clothing, surroundings, and food. They listened to the wisdom of their bodies by moving less intensely, seeking movement for grounding and release. They selected foods that were clean and light so as to limit internal inflammation and heat. Their community honored our foremothers during this time by not approaching them with new ideas or lists of demands. They were given space and time to meet their own needs while meeting the needs of their family and friends.

In this way, using the gifts bestowed to them as daughters of Gaia, our grandmother's grandmothers lived a life of deep connection, balance, and harmony. Honoring their rhythm and the rhythms of their sisters, they practiced and modeled self-care throughout their cycles, and throughout their lives. This wild wisdom, this gift to all daughters of Gaia, may not have been shared with us through our matriline; it may have been hidden and buried and denied for generations. But it *is* ours, sisters; it is our birthright, coded into our very DNA; it is ours to reclaim.

With a final deep inhale and exhale, allow yourself to connect fully to your own deep wisdom, the wisdom of the Sacred Feminine, and know that you can access this powerful connection at any time. With gentle awareness of your body now, you begin to shift back into the present moment. Moving with ease, you are once again in the here and now. Welcome back!

FOR DEEPER REFLECTION

What cultural messages have you internalized about the "seasonal" shifts of your hormonal cycle?

In what ways are you currently preventing yourself from experiencing the powerful gifts of your monthly rhythm?

What would it feel like to give yourself permission to know yourself as the sacred manifestation of Mother Nature?

This meditation was inspired by the book 4 Seasons in 4 Weeks *by Suzanne Mathis McQueen.*

REBIRTH & RENEWAL

stara, the ancient Germanic Goddess of Rebirth and Renewal, is our modern-day maiden of springtime and the namesake of the Easter holiday. With her iconic rabbit and colorful eggs, Ostara heralds the rebirth of the Earth and her creatures, inviting us to reflect upon our own personal experience of renewal. Pushing through the growing pains of evolution can sometimes feel daunting, but when we allow ourselves to embody the wild wisdom of Ostara, we connect with a deep source of spiritual potential and promise.

MEDITATION

Imagine lying in the soil, dormant, resting, healing, gathering strength and inspiration. Feel the support of the soil all around you, cradling you. You feel so safe and cozy here in your flower bed.

Speaking directly to your core, you hear a voice that says, "Hello beloved. I am Ostara, Goddess of Rebirth and Renewal." As you hear these words, Ostara sends an image of herself into your mind's eye. You see and notice everything about her; what she looks like, what she is wearing, and you notice that she lovingly cradles an egg in her hands.

Ostara tells you, "I have come with the loving message

that it is time to wake up! Time to blossom, time to shine, and to grow the good medicine of your unique gifts. No flower, tree, or plant is like another; they each have their own signature energy that they were created to share.

"Each winter, you rest in stillness, preparing yourself by focusing your intentions, and reflecting on the wisdom of past cycles.

"It is spring, and this year, as in all years that have come before, you are reborn, inspired to nurture and cultivate your medicine. Each turn of the wheel is another cycle to practice, to learn, to grow, and to wisely shed what no longer serves you so that your precious resources serve only your highest good.

"And now, beautiful spirit, flame of creation, I invite you to reawaken. Hear me now, my beloved, as I sing the song of your medicine. Hear my blessing upon your body and spirit as I beckon you to push through... though your fear and your doubt may weigh heavily upon you, you can push through to the light... you can push through to the beauty of renewal, as you birth yourself into the fullness of your being once more."

FOR DEEPER REFLECTION

What cultural messages have you internalized about the experience of renewal?

In what ways are you currently preventing yourself from moving through the process of rebirth?

What would it feel like to give yourself permission to align with the potency of spring renewal?

TENDING YOUR
INNER GARDEN

Our inner garden is the metaphorical internal land-scape that serves as the cradle for the spiritual and creative seeds of intention we plant each winter solstice. It is our own personal microcosm of manifestation, subject to the same whims of nature – including unwelcome invasive species. Even the most seasoned spiritual seeker must cultivate a regular practice of tending her inner garden, bring awareness to her self-defeating thoughts and negative inner narratives: the weeds of this sacred terrain. When we allow ourselves to align with the wild and wise flow of the Wheel of the Year, we offer ourselves the opportunity to bring loving awareness to the health of our interior biomes and ensure the expression of our most sacred potential.

MEDITATION

Take a deep breath and as you exhale, allow your gaze to completely relax. On your next inhale, allow your eyes to close and shift your attention to your inner garden – the home of the seeds of intention you planted at the winter solstice and encouraged to bloom during spring.

Notice every detail of this beautiful ecosystem; this microcosm of creation. Take note of what has emerged from the soil already – what has pushed through toward the light, what is blooming and ripening. Take a moment to give yourself gratitude for the inner work you have done thus far during the year.

As you survey this lovely scene, you can't help but notice that among the beautiful flowers blossoming, there are some weeds crowding their way in. Easy to overlook amongst the abundance of your garden, these weeds indeed impede the growth of the seeds you have planted, by leeching nutrients from your soil, hoarding water, and simply taking up space. Unwelcome and unbidden, the weeds prevent your inner garden from realizing its full potential.

Knowing that the peak of summer is when we are invited to reflect and release, you feel inspired to tend to your inner garden by weeding out the thoughts, beliefs, feelings, and patterns that no longer serve you.

Observing your inner garden now, give yourself permission to see and name the weeds that are crowding out the seeds that you've planted.

What thoughts or beliefs or patterns are you ready to be rid of?

The weeds in our inner garden represent anything that hinders or limits us from becoming the full, radiant beings we are meant to be.

Are you stuck in an old story about your body?

Do you repeat and reinforce an attitude of scarcity?

Does your notion of age, or education level, or family history hold you back from realizing your true potential?

Does your relationship with food, or caffeine, or sugar deplete your resources rather than nourish your system?

Take a moment now to use your inner gaze to see and name the weeds in your garden. You may choose to write them down now or when this meditation is finished.

Back in your inner realm, it is time to begin your practice of release by removing those weeds.

See them. Name them. And then grab them and pull them out of the ground. Throw them into the fire and watch them burn.

With a deep inhale and exhale, thank yourself for this devoted practice of self-care and self-love.

Returning your attention to your garden, you note that yes, the weeds are gone in this moment. But like any weed in any garden, you can expect them to come back. Such is the nature of weeds.

The process of tending your inner garden involves checking in regularly and pulling out those weeds – some of which can be very stubborn – and at the same time, nourishing your soil to encourage your seeds of intention to continue to flourish. What nourishment does your garden need in order to thrive?

Imagine your garden now, in full bloom. Feel yourself growing stronger, more radiant, and more joyful as your seeds of intention reach their full potential. With your devotion to self-care as you tend to your inner garden, the sky is the limit!

FOR DEEPER REFLECTION

What cultural messages have you internalized about self-talk?

In what ways are you currently preventing yourself from thriving?

What would it feel like to give yourself permission to blossom into your full potential?

THANK YOU

ultivating and safekeeping a core of deep self-worth and self-appreciation is truly the wellspring of our self-care practice. If we lack a sense of our own deserving, our self-care will never feel authentic or take priority in our lives. When we pause to honor the things for which we so richly deserve our own gratitude and appreciation, we make space to begin reclaiming the wild and wise Sacred Feminine truth that we are enough.

MEDITATION

Take a deep breath in and allow yourself to relax completely as you exhale. Sense the ground beneath you, supporting you, and feel the cool breath of autumn as it whispers through the crimson canopy of leaves above you. As the wheel of the year shifts from the full bloom of our abundant summer to the crisp days of fall, we are invited to consciously take inventory of the many seeds of intention that have bloomed to fruition throughout the year.

Now is the time of year to reflect with gratitude... but not only for all the amazing things that have happened to us, or for the love that others have offered us. In addition to all of this, we can tune in with the waves of gratitude that we ourselves deserve.

As women, we are not conditioned to reflect upon *and own* all of the amazing things that we do each and every day; we are not taught to acknowledge our strength, our power, our wisdom, our perseverance. We are not invited to inventory all of the times we made the next right choice and acted from love instead of fear. All of the times we pushed through, pressed on, and persisted.

But today, we will do exactly that.

I now invite you to open your journal for a writing meditation.

At the top of one blank page, you will write "Thank you for…"

At the top of the next blank page, you will write, "I am so thankful that you…"

At the top of the next blank page, you will write, "I know it wasn't easy for you to…"

And at the top of the next blank page, you will write, "You showed up for me when you…"

Allow yourself to spend as much time as you need to complete the gratitude prompts on each page.

When you have completed your writing, take time to give voice to all of your gratitude affirmations aloud. Speaking as a beloved friend, acknowledge to yourself all that you have done from this place of self-love, self-worth, and self-respect.

With a last deep breath in, take a moment to feel the deep resonance of your gratitude; bring awareness to how you feel right now. This feeling is yours to claim at any time, your birthright. Make a commitment to revisit this practice regularly, and remember your affirmations whenever you need to tap into your deep appreciation for yourself. You gently begin now to return to this present moment, to this space and time. Welcome back!

FOR DEEPER REFLECTION

What cultural messages have you internalized about your self-worth?

In what ways are you currently preventing yourself from offering yourself appreciation and love?

What would it feel like to give yourself permission to speak to yourself the way you would speak to a beloved friend?

PREPARING FOR THE DARK

Autumn is the natural time to shift out of the frenzied time of productivity, and to begin to reflect on the seasons that have passed. We can look back with gratitude on the seeds that we planted earlier this year and acknowledge the fruits of our labors, knowing that winter will soon invite us to slow our pace and rest in preparation for the year ahead. When we give ourselves permission to truly appreciate the wild wisdom of darkness as much as we do the light, we honor our inherent cycle of waxing and waning and our innate Sacred Feminine rhythm.

MEDITATION

Allow yourself to relax fully, and find your breath. Sink deep into the Earth, knowing you are completely supported. Connect with your heartbeat, and feel waves of relaxation pass through your body with each pulse.

Feel your body lying on the ground, outside, in a sacred and safe place. Notice how your body feels... notice what you hear and sense around you. It is twilight, and you are aware that the last remnants of daylight are fading into the inky black sky. Darkness is coming.

But not just the darkness of the coming night... no; you are also aware of the darkness that comes with the turning of the Wheel of the Year. Deep into autumn now, you sense that winter will soon be on her way. The daylight hours grow scarce as the nights seem to stretch on and on... we rise in the dark each morning, and it is dark again by dinner.

Take a moment now to observe your physical, emotional, and spiritual response to this coming of the darkness.

The natural world around us responds as a matter of course to this shifting, to the waning that must follow the full ripeness of summer. Leaves change and fall, crops go to rest. Animals work hard to put on fat and store their provisions for winter's scarcity. Safe dens are made cozy and warm for stillness and rest. Preparations are made: it is instinctual.

And what of us? What preparations do we make for the coming of this darkness, sisters?

Do we... make our lists and check them twice? Do we add even more to the pile of expectations we place upon ourselves? Do we ramp up our perfectionism in the face of Pinterest and Martha Stewart and the memory of last year's magazine-worthy holiday cards that came in the mail?

Does our instinct to hoard compel us to buy and collect even more in the material world, rather than focusing on shoring up our emotional and spiritual reserves? Do we know how to heed – or even *hear* – the voice of Pachamama, telling us that now is the time to cultivate stillness, to prioritize quiet, to shift our gaze inward?

Late fall is the natural time to shift out of the frenzied time of productivity, and to begin to reflect on the seasons that have passed. We can look back with gratitude on the seeds that we planted earlier this year and acknowledge the fruits of our labors, knowing that *this* season invites us to slow our pace and rest in preparation for the year ahead.

In this way – the way of the Sacred Feminine – we honor our inherent cycle of waxing and waning. We feel and experience the rhythm of the Mother… we know just exactly how we can best prepare for the coming of the dark.

FOR DEEPER REFLECTION

What cultural messages have you internalized about late fall and winter (particularly the holidays)?

In what ways are you currently preventing yourself from experiencing the wisdom of winter?

What would it feel like to give yourself permission to spend some time in energetic and spiritual hibernation?

WINTER SPIRAL

he custom of setting new year's intentions on January 1st is no doubt the Gregorian appropriation of traditional winter solstice ceremonies. The longest night is indeed a potent time to pause and reflect on the year that has passed, releasing what no longer serves us in order to make space for our seeds of intention for the upcoming year. When we align with the Wheel of the Year and flow with wild wisdom of the solstice, we invite ourselves to dwell thoughtfully in the close comfort of the womb-like darkness, and make preparations for the rebirth of the sun.

MEDITATION

Take a deep breath and exhale completely, sinking into deep relaxation. You feel completely still in this darkness, breathing naturally. As you orient yourself to your surroundings, you feel the cold, crisp air of this winter night, and you see your breath as you exhale. You feel a candle in your hand, though it is not yet lit.

In the distance, you notice a bonfire, and you walk toward it. You hear the crunch of your feet through the snow, and you know instinctively: this is winter solstice, the longest night. As you approach the fire, you see that it is encircled by a beautiful evergreen bough spiral, adorned with twelve unlit luminarias, white candles set in simple paper bags, from the center to the edge.

You follow your heart's calling to step into the spiral, and know that this walk through the spiral to the center fire is a time of reverent reflection: a time to pause and look back upon the year that is now coming to an end.

As you take a deep breath in, you see that the first luminaria candle, which represents this past January, is suddenly lit – as if by magic. You step into the spiral and gaze into the soft light of this first candle, and remember back to the first month of the year. What stands out as most memorable? Is there a word that best encapsulates the energy and feelings of January? Is there anything you'd like to tuck away and hold onto from January?

When you feel complete in your reflection of January, the next luminaria begins to glow. You walk further into the spiral until you are standing before the second candle, and reflect upon the month of February. What memories are most vivid? Is there a word that best encapsulates the energy and feelings of February? What lessons from February will you hold onto?

When you feel complete in your reflection of February, the next luminaria begins to glow. You walk further into the spiral until you are standing before the third candle, and reflect upon the month of March. What stands out as most memorable? Is there a word that best encapsulates the energy and feelings of March? Is there anything you'd like to tuck away and hold onto from March?

When you feel complete in your reflection of March, the fourth luminaria begins to glow. You walk further into the spiral until you are standing before the candle for the month of April. What memories are most vivid? Is there a word that best encapsulates the energy and feelings of April? What lessons from April will you hold onto?

When you feel complete in your reflection of April, the next luminaria begins to glow. You walk further into the spiral until you are standing before the fifth candle, and reflect upon the month of May. What stands out as most memorable? Is there a word that best encapsulates the energy and feelings of May? Is there anything you'd like to tuck away and hold onto from May?

When you feel complete in your reflection of May, you step further into the spiral and stand in front of the sixth candle, pondering the month of June. What memories are most vivid? Is there a word that best encapsulates the energy and feelings of June? What lessons from June will you hold onto?

Halfway through the year now, you notice you are stepping ever closer to the fire at the center of the spiral, still holding your unlit candle as the seventh luminaria begins to glow. You pause here and reflect on the past summer, the shift in energy that comes with the turning of the wheel of the year, and remember the month of July. What stands out as most memorable? Is there a word that best encapsulates the energy and feelings of July? Is there anything you'd like to tuck away and hold onto from the first month of summer?

When you feel complete in your reflection of July, the eighth luminaria begins to glow. You walk further into the spiral until you are standing before the candle for the month of August. What memories are most vivid? Is there a word that best encapsulates the energy and feelings of August? What lessons from August will you hold onto?

When you feel complete in your reflection of August,

you step further into the spiral and stand in front of the ninth luminaria, pondering the month of September. What memories are most vivid? Is there a word that best encapsulates the energy and feelings of summer's end? What lessons from September will you hold onto?

When you feel complete in your reflection of September, you step further into the spiral and notice you are nearing the center fire, and there are only three luminarias ahead. The tenth luminaria begins to glow, inviting you to reflect upon the month of October. What memories are most vivid? Is there a word that best encapsulates the energy and feelings of the shift into fall? What lessons from October will you hold onto?

When you feel complete in your reflection of October, the eleventh luminaria – only steps from the center fire – begins to glow. You walk further into the spiral until you are standing before the luminaria for the month of November. What memories are most vivid? Is there a word that best encapsulates the energy and feelings of November? What lessons from November will you hold onto?

When you feel complete in your reflection of November, the twelfth and final luminaria begins to glow. You step to the center of the spiral until you are standing before the luminaria for the month of December with the bonfire just before you. What memories are most vivid for this final month of the year? Is there a word that best encapsulates the energy and feelings of December? What lessons or accomplishments from December will you hold onto?

With a deep inhale and exhale, you offer your gratitude for the memories, accomplishments, and lessons of this year. You stand for a moment and observe the stunning beauty of the fire in front of you, and the evergreen spiral that surrounds you. Your heart fills at the sight of the twelve luminarias, now aglow with your memories and wisdom.

Your focus returns to the fire that you now stand before, and you shift your thoughts toward the year ahead. With the completion of this year now sealed by your spiral walk, you know that it is time to begin to plant your seeds of intention for the coming year. You look deep within yourself, finding that your spirit knows exactly which seeds to plant.

You reach down and light the candle that you've held during this journey, feeling the warmth of the bonfire, and know that this warmth will sustain your fragile seeds through the dormancy of winter.

You hold this candle with both hands now, the flame in front of your heart, and your word or phrase for the coming year arises naturally from your spirit. This will be the mantra that you return to: your anchor-point that will allow your seeds of intention to take root and bloom in their full radiance in the year ahead.

You repeat your mantra, saying it out loud into the dark night, and feel it resonate perfectly in your body and soul. With a final nod of gratitude for the fire and the night, you turn and begin your journey back out of the spiral, focusing not on the year behind, but the year to come.

When you have reached the end of the spiral, you take one final breath in, and as you exhale, you begin your journey back into your body. With gentle ease, you begin to move slowly, finding your way back to this time and place. When you are ready, open your eyes. Welcome back!

FOR DEEPER REFLECTION

What cultural messages have you internalized about the ending of the year?

In what ways are you currently preventing yourself from experiencing the cyclical nature of time?

What would it feel like to give yourself permission to pause and release at the turn of each year?

Read by the author, the WILD & WISE audiobook
is also available on CD and on Audible.

ABOUT THE AUTHOR

Amy Bammel Wilding is the founder of Red Tent Louisville, a sacred interfaith women's community. She has been leading sacred women's circles, mother-daughter circles and retreats, and rite-of-passage ceremonies since 2006, just after her initiation to motherhood. The pregnancy and birth of her daughter in 2005 catalyzed her evolution by setting her on a path toward healing and Sacred Feminism, and sparked her passion for empowering women by helping them to reclaim their inherent power and wisdom.

Amy is a perpetual student of womanhood and spirituality, and is continually inspired by the place where the two realms overlap. Called to share her medicine with girls and women throughout the lifespan, she is a trained and loving guide in the areas of the Goddess archetype, sacred self-care, sexuality education, maidenhood, grief and loss, breastfeeding, and the menstrual cycle. Passionate about empowering girls and women, Amy is devoted to witnessing and inspiring the reawakening of the Sacred Feminine from the individual to the global level. She offers women's circle leadership training as well as private mentorship and private event facilitation.

Connect with Amy via email at amy@redtentlouisville.com or on her website, www.redtentlouisville.com

ABOUT THE COVER ARTIST

Sally J. Smith is an artist based in the Adirondack Mountains, NY, USA. A professional watercolor artist of over 25 years, in 2007 she began creating environmental art sculptures out in nature.

"My 'Eartherials' are a pure celebration of the materials and the environment itself. Spirals are the backbone design form I like to work with and they are created out of everything imaginable: ice, stones, flowers, leaves and water itself on occasion.

"The process is usually rather mysterious. Sometimes it begins with an idea, or an inner prompting to work with a particular landscape or material. Always what is required is a deep sensitivity to the rhythms of the land, the seasonal shifts and the flight of the sun or moon across the sky. One enters the creative process the same way one enters a secret glade in the forest – quietly and with reverence. Keeping the lines of communication open between myself and whatever natural forces may be present in the environment allows me to see more deeply into a moment in space and time and endeavor to create a work of art that arises out of this mystery."

www.greenspiritarts.com

ALSO FROM WOMANCRAFT PUBLISHING

Burning Woman

Lucy H. Pearce

ISBN 978-1910559-161

Uncompromising and all-encompassing, Pearce uncovers the archetype of the Burning Women of days gone by through to the way women are burned today, fearlessly examining the roots of Feminine power – what it is, how it has been controlled, and why it needs to be unleashed on the world during our modern Burning Times.

Lucy H. Pearce's Burning Woman carries the torch of the sacred Feminine into the dark corners of women's unexpressed and unfulfilled desire and power. She dares us to burn down that which does not serve life, to use our fire to transform the world.

Oriah 'Mountain Dreamer' House

Moon Time: harness the ever-changing energy of your menstrual cycle

Lucy H. Pearce

Amazon #1 bestseller in Menstruation ISBN 978-1910559-062

Hailed as 'life-changing' by women around the world, *Moon Time* shares a fully embodied understanding of the menstrual cycle. Full of practical insight, empowering resources, creative activities and passion, this book will put women back in touch with their body's wisdom.

Lucy, your book is monumental. The wisdom in Moon Time sets a new course where we glimpse a future culture reshaped by honoring our womanhood journeys one woman at a time.

ALisa Starkweather, author and founder of Red Tent Temple

The Heart of the Labyrinth

Nicole Schwab

ISBN 978-1910559-000

Reminiscent of Paulo Coelho's masterpiece *The Alchemist* and Lynn V. Andrew's acclaimed *Medicine Woman* series, *The Heart of the Labyrinth* is a beautifully evocative spiritual parable, filled with exotic landscapes and transformational soul lessons.

Once in a while, a book comes along that kindles the fire of our inner wisdom so profoundly, the words seem to leap off the page and go straight into our heart. If you read only one book this year, this is it.

Dean Ornish, M.D, President, Preventive Medicine Research Institute, Author of *The Spectrum*

The Other Side of the River: Stories of Women, Water and the World

Eila Kundrie Carrico

ISBN 978-1910559-185

Rooted in rivers, inspired by wetlands, sources and tributaries, this book weaves its path between the banks of memory and story, from Florida to Kyoto, storm-ravaged New Orleans to London, via San Francisco and Ghana. We navigate through flood and drought to confront the place of wildness in the age of technology. A deep searching into the ways we become dammed and how we recover fluidity. A journey through memory and time, personal and shared landscapes to discover the source, the flow and the deltas of women and water.

An instant classic for the new paradigm.

Lucia Chiavola Birnbaum, award-winning author and Professor Emeritus

Dirty & Divine: a transformative journey through tarot
Alice B. Grist

ISBN: 978-1910559-253

There is something sacred within you, in all that you are and all that you do. In a mix of you that is everyday dirty, and spiritually divine, there is something so perfect, something more. Whether beginner or seasoned tarot practitioner, *Dirty & Divine* is written to accompany you on a powerful personal intuitive journey to plumb the depths of your existence and encompass the spectrum of wisdom that the cards can offer, a tarot-led vision quest to reclaiming your femininity in all its lucid and colorful depths.

Alice has been my go-to woman for tarot readings for years now, because her truth, knowledge + wisdom are the REAL DEAL.
Lisa Lister, author of *Love your Lady Landscape*

Moods of Motherhood: the inner journey of mothering
Lucy H. Pearce

ISBN 978-1910559-031

Giving voice to the often nebulous, unspoken tumble of emotions that motherhood evokes: tenderness, frustration, joy, grief, anger, depression and love, Pearce explores the taboo subjects of maternal ambiguity, competitiveness, and the quest for perfection, offering support, acceptance, and hope to mothers everywhere.

Lucy's frank and forthright style paired with beautiful, haunting language and her talent for storytelling will have any parent nodding, crying and laughing along – appreciating the good and the bad, the hard and the soft, the light and the dark. A must-read for any new parent.
Zoe Foster, *JUNO* magazine

Full Circle Health: integrated health charting for women
Lucy H. Pearce

ISBN 978-1910559-222

A creative approach to holistic health for all who love planners, trackers and bullet journals to guide and support you in a greater understanding of your physical, mental and emotional health.

Whether menstruating or not, pregnant or post-partum, *Full Circle Health* provides a highly flexible, deeply supportive way of tracking your health, whatever your current health conditions.

With 35 daily charting spreads, a monthly habit tracker, planner, and charting grid, this integrated tool will help you to track symptoms, medication, self-care, energy levels, build positive health habits and mindful awareness.

The Heroines Club: A Mother-Daughter Empowerment Circle
Melia Keeton-Digby

ISBN 978-1910559-147

Nourishing guidance and a creative approach for mothers and daughters, aged 7+, to learn and grow together through the study of women's history. Each month focuses on a different heroine, featuring athletes, inventors, artists, and revolutionaries from around the world – including Frida Kahlo, Rosalind Franklin, Amelia Earhart, Anne Frank, Maya Angelou and Malala Yousafzai as strong role models for young girls to learn about, look up to, and be inspired by.

The Heroines Club is truly a must-have book for mothers who wish to foster a deeper connection with their daughters. As mothers, we are our daughter's first teacher, role model, and wise counsel. This book should be in every woman's hands, and passed down from generation to generation.

Wendy Cook, founder and facilitator of Mighty Girl Art

Womancraft
PUBLISHING

Life-changing, paradigm-shifting books
by women, for women

WWW.WOMANCRAFTPUBLISHING.COM

Sign up to the mailing list for discounts and see
samples of forthcoming titles before anyone else.

(f) WomancraftPublishing

(y) WomancraftBooks

(o) Womancraft_Publishing

If you have enjoyed this book, please leave a review
at your favorite retailer or Goodreads.

14860566R00102